KITCHENS
FOR COOKS

∎ ∎ ∎

PLANNING YOUR PERFECT KITCHEN

ALSO BY DEBORAH KRASNER

■ ■ ■

Celtic: Design and Style in Homes of Scotland, Ireland, and Wales

From Celtic Hearths: Baked Goods from Scotland, Ireland, and Wales

Heirloom Skills and Country Pastimes:
Traditional Projects for Kitchen, Home, Garden, and Family

KITCHENS FOR COOKS

PLANNING YOUR PERFECT KITCHEN

DEBORAH KRASNER

■ ■ ■

PHOTOGRAPHS BY WILLIAM STITES

DRAWINGS BY JOHN R. PAOLI ARCHITECTS

DESIGN BY KATHLEEN HERLIHY-PAOLI

PENGUIN STUDIO

PENGUIN STUDIO
Published by the Penguin Group
Penguin Books USA Inc., 375 Hudson Street,
New York, New York 10014, U.S.A.
Penguin Books Ltd, 27 Wrights Lane,
London W8 5TZ, England
Penguin Books Australia Ltd, Ringwood,
Victoria, Australia
Penguin Books Canada Ltd, 10 Alcorn Avenue,
Toronto, Ontario, Canada M4V 3B2
Penguin Books (N.Z.) Ltd, 182–190 Wairau Road,
Auckland 10, New Zealand

Penguin Books Ltd, Registered Offices:
Harmondsworth, Middlesex, England

First published by Viking Studio Books,
an imprint of Viking Penguin,
a division of Penguin Books USA Inc.1994
Penguin Studio edition published 1996

1 3 5 7 9 10 8 6 4 2

ISBN 0 14 02.4811 0

CIP data available

Printed in Singapore

Designed by Kathleen Herlihy-Paoli

THIS BOOK IS DEDICATED TO MY PARENTS

■ ■ ■

My father, David Shapiro, taught me about design in everyday life and spent Sunday mornings making blueberry muffins; my mother, Cecile Shapiro, wrote our family's first kitchen book both in word and in deed.

ACKNOWLEDGMENTS

■ ■ ■

These days, Michael, Abby, and Lizzie teach me how to share space with multiple cooks, and I am grateful for their cooking as well as their company.

I am also grateful to many friends and acquaintances for their help: Lisa and Lou Ekus, Rondi Lightmark and Jim Chapman, Nadav Malin, Liz Blum, Amy Bernhardt, Shoshana Rihn, Eco-sentials, Gloria Levitas, Kevin Connelly, and each of the home owners featured in this book, who deepen and enrich our sense of what kitchens can be.

Thank you also to Barbara Williams and Michael Fragnito at Viking Studio Books, to Amy Berkower of Writers House, to Kathy Herlihy-Paoli and John R. Paoli of Inkstone Design, and to photographer Bill Stites for collectively making such a great team. I feel lucky to be on it.

CONTENTS

■

PART I

LOOKING CLOSELY AT KITCHENS: A FUNCTIONAL APPROACH

■

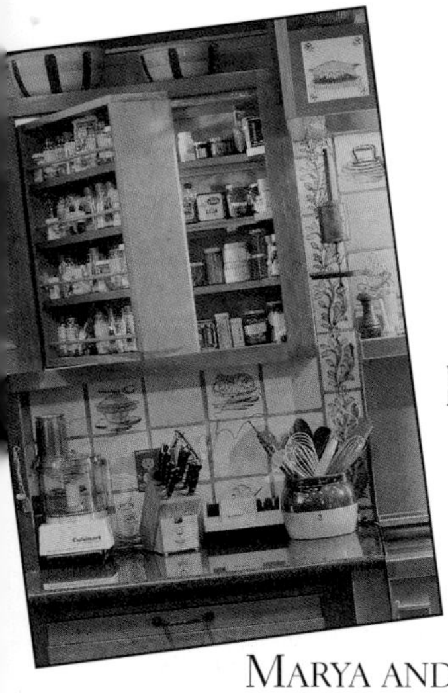

PART II

REAL COOKS, WORKING KITCHENS

AVID HOME COOKS

COOKBOOK AUTHORS AT HOME

RESTAURANT CHEFS

CATERERS

■

PART III

SOURCES

KITCHENS FOR COOKS

. . .

PLANNING <u>YOUR</u> PERFECT KITCHEN

INTRODUCTION

I WANTED TO WRITE THIS BOOK BECAUSE I FELT THAT MOST KITCHEN designs were based on a sexist and outmoded assumption—that kitchens were the province of one well-aproned woman, cooking alone in a particularly Mrs. Cleaverish, meatloaf-and-mashed-potato way. In researching this book I then discovered that in fact the news is even worse than that! *Kitchens as we know them are actually designed for a 5-foot-9-inch-tall scientist who probably doesn't do much real cooking anyway!*

Another motivating factor for me was the realization that the work spaces and traffic patterns in my own kitchen didn't work as well as they should, especially when children, spouse, and friends were cooking together. I wanted to discover how to create kitchens that really work for people who enjoy the process of cooking, particularly when there is more than one cook in the kitchen at a time.

As I started this research, I was struck (once I got beyond surface style and color) by how similar the basic traffic and work patterns and overall designs of kitchens were, whether they were in rural northern California or the Upper East Side of Manhattan. Judging from many of the magazines and books I've been seeing, one would think that somehow our ideal of what a kitchen should look like has little relation to geography, access to food sources, size and composition of household, or the seasons and climates.

It seems to me that we've been designing kitchens for looks, for show, and for status, and less and less for real use. Of course, many of those same magazines have been telling us a few contradictory things about kitchens. On the one hand, we've been hearing a lot about (and seeing) kitchens as the new "heart of the house," as the new (again) central or great room. And in new construction, we see a trend emerging—the size of the kitchens grows as the living room shrinks.

On the other hand, we hear about (and see) families who rarely get a chance to sit down and eat together, much less cook for one another. For these harried grazers, the kitchen can be seen as wasted space or window dressing, in much the same way that many people now see formal dining rooms.

Lending further credence to the notion that kitchens are obsolete, most American families have microwaves, which they use to reheat purchased frozen entrées as well as take-out meals. And we see a new proliferation of establishments that prepare whole meals for those with "no time to cook."

Because our country encompasses great extremes of climate; because our needs and desires for kitchen work space are so various; because our limitations of architecture and budget range from enormous to modest—doesn't it make sense to think about and create kitchens that really suit our different needs?

The purpose of this book is to give people some new ways of thinking about their ideal kitchen, and to help them figure out what options they want to consider, and how to include them. This is not a how-to book. Rather, it is a "how-to-think-about" book designed to provide ideas for creating well-planned and comfortable kitchens. Such personal, well-fitting, and idiosyncratic spaces can only enhance our ability to work well within them.

To that end, we will look at kitchens functionally, examining cooking the way professional chefs do, from the perspective of preparation areas. We'll look at storage needs and space needs, as well as surfaces and style, thinking first about what is needed and what works, and last about how it looks.

Finally, we will examine real kitchens of working cooks, whether they are avid home cooks, restaurant chefs, cooking teachers, cooking authors, or caterers, asking the people who spend more than ordinary time in their kitchens what works and what doesn't, and why.

PART ONE

LOOKING CLOSELY AT KITCHENS

...

A FUNCTIONAL APPROACH

KITCHENS THAT FUNCTION WELL FOR MANY COOKS AT ONCE ARE often those that have nothing at all to do with that magic work triangle we've been hearing so much about for the last thirty years. Instead, they have well-thought-out areas for different kinds of food preparation.

The best models for multiple work stations and separate preparation areas are restaurant kitchens. In these professional kitchens, years of tradition and planning have gone into setting up efficient cooking areas for different tasks. There are separate stations for salad prep; for grilling, baking, and roasting; for sautéing and for pastry making. There are saucier stations, and a plating area for artful food arranging and for serving. Because home kitchens function with a smaller and less skilled cooking staff, even if everyone is involved in the process, I've simplified work stations into WET/DRY/HOT/COLD, which are categories, or zones, that make more sense to me.

Organizing by function, or preparation area, is a unique way of thinking about the design of a new kitchen because it breaks down preconceived ideas about appearance and placement that can often get in the way of intelligent planning.

I also feel that there are other design assumptions that need questioning: Why should kitchens look streamlined? Why not use different countertop materials in different parts of the kitchen where they would make sense (tile near the stove, butcher block on the prep counters, laminate near the sinks, marble at the pastry prep)? Why use overhead closed cabinets, when open shelving, as in restaurants, often makes so much more sense? Why hide so much of the equipment we need to cook with, when having it all accessible would be more efficient?

And in thinking about making a functional kitchen that will both transcend style and work well for many years to come, it is important, I feel, to emphasize the

Green choices we can make in our daily lives. Much of the resources we waste are kitchen-related, whether food, packaging, or nonrenewable energy; but it is also relatively easy to train ourselves to deal with this waste more sensitively when we have provided spaces in which to do so. I have included ideas in the text and references in the Source Guide to help others make those choices.

WET ZONE

WET PREPARATION REFERS TO A FAIRLY MUNDANE SET OF KITCHEN activities, such as peeling carrots or washing lettuce, all of which take place in or near a sink. It is essential to plan for traffic and work space to accommodate these functions and their ancillary equipment. WET also includes cleanup tasks, such as dishwashing. In planning the location of the WET zone, make sure to create a clear path from the dining table to the sink and dirty-dish area. Leave a large (18- to 36-inch) space for clearing dishes on one side of the sink and a similar space for draining clean dishes on the other side.

WET STORAGE

What is most conveniently stored near WET? It makes sense to store everyday glassware and china as close to the sink and dishwasher as possible. There are a number of ways to accomplish this: open shelves, wall-mounted dish drainer and racks, closed cupboards that are conveniently located, and/or decorative plate racks.

Similarly, all machines in daily use that need water (electric coffee makers and electric tea kettles) should be located near the sink. Any auxiliary equipment for such machines needs to be stored nearby—the coffee grinder, for example, along with paper filters, tea bags or canisters, and the coffee thermos or teapot. Other tools that often have water added to them (blender, food processor, electric rice cooker, mixer) could also be usefully accommodated near the sink, either on the countertop, in an appliance garage or cabinet, or on a "pull-up" shelf that is fitted into a base cabinet and rises to counter height.

Each of these small WET-related appliances generates electrical requirements. Since you will be putting in at least one electrical box here for the dishwasher, be sure to add in a long row of plugs (at least six) along the backsplash for appliance use.

The simplest way to create an appliance-holding counter area is to add 6 inches to the depth of a wall-hugging counter that covers a standard base cabinet (this means setting the cabinet out 6 inches from the wall). This additional depth can accommodate a row of countertop appliances ranged along the back wall without compromising the available counter work space.

The next logical step would be to hide these appliances from view by enclosing them behind doors in an "appliance garage." Another solution to getting larger appliances out of sight is to store them on pull-up sections of under-cabinet shelves, each fitted with hardware that enables the appliance—a heavy mixer, for example— to rise to countertop level.

More streamlined still is an integral multi-use appliance base wired into the counter, such as NuTone's kitchen machine. Even such almost-integral solutions, however, create storage requirements for attachments when not in use.

Storage for WET also includes nonelectric tools that are used to drain liquids, such as a salad spinner or colander. It makes sense to locate these items in a nearby drawer or cabinet that is handy to a sink.

The sink itself creates storage requirements as well as storage capacity underneath. You need to plan a space for dishwashing soaps (machine and hand), scouring pads and cleansers, bottle brushes, rubber gloves, hand cream, and whatever else you require for WET cleaning tasks.

Other cleaning supplies for the kitchen—bucket, broom, mop, sponges, rags, jars, and spray bottles—are best stored in a broom closet. If you live with a child or a puppy, you'll want this area to be above waist-level, or provided with a lock.

Finally, if you have the space, consider an old-fashioned butler's pantry for auxiliary storage in the WET zone. While I don't know anyone with a butler, I know lots of people who could use more room outside the main kitchen traffic area for storage of china, serving dishes, table linen, silverware, and special occasion cookware and tableware. Because this pantry was also designed as a place for maintaining those objects, it traditionally included a sink for polishing silver and washing china.

WET EQUIPMENT
(BUILT-IN AND FIXED)

SINKS

There is an enormous variety of sinks on the market—large and small; single, double, and triple; of stainless steel, brass, enameled cast iron, acrylics and composites such as Corian, and cast lightweight concrete. It is still possible to find shallow old stone sinks in salvage yards and antiques shops, as well as to have copper, stainless-steel, or ceramic sinks fabricated in custom sizes. Many of the cooks featured in this book have either chosen the largest-size standard sinks, or have had undermounted sinks custom-made. Others have chosen antique stone sinks, both for reasons of sentiment and for their often-generous size.

Sink materials and style are very much a matter of personal preference. Of the two most commonly chosen sink materials—enameled cast iron and stainless steel—enameled cast iron is extremely durable, is available in a variety of colors (that sometimes have a tendency to fade), and will definitely break or chip any dish that may slip from your soapy grasp.

Stainless-steel sinks are available with various chromium/nickel ratios, and are priced accordingly. The best are supposed to have an 18/10 ratio of chromium to nickel, be smooth rather than brushed, and have a satin finish rather than a mirror finish. Stainless always scratches and spots (even the most expensive, no matter

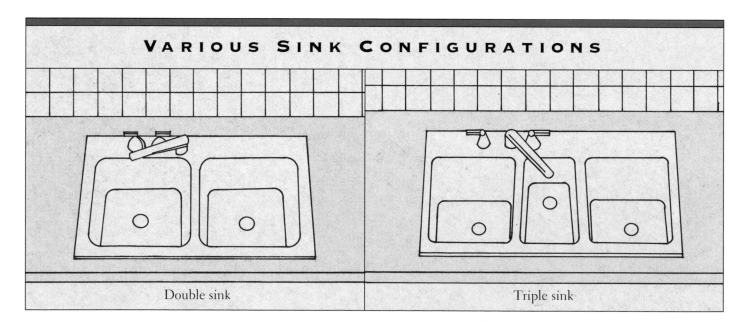

VARIOUS SINK CONFIGURATIONS

| Double sink | Triple sink |

what the manufacturers promise in their sales literature), and it always needs drying and/or polishing. The best stainless, however, is much less prone to denting, and the difference in quality is apparent. All stainless-steel sinks are gentle on china and glassware.

Some of the new synthetic sinks have colors that don't fade, and surfaces that are not so hard that dishes almost always break when dropped. When such sinks are designed as an integral part of the countertop, they eliminate those irritating hard-to-clean cracks between sink and counter. It's possible, and worth considering if your kitchen budget is second-mortgage-size, to have an integral sink and wall-mounted faucets, thus creating a WET area without any places that need to be scrubbed with a fingernail.

If your sink isn't integral, plan to buy one that installs flush-mounted or undermounted (below the level of your countertop). If there is an option in your chosen material and price range, the best sink is always an undermounted one, because its placement eliminates areas for dirt and water to collect on the countertop. It also provides the most streamlined appearance.

The size of the sink matters. The best advice I know is to take your largest

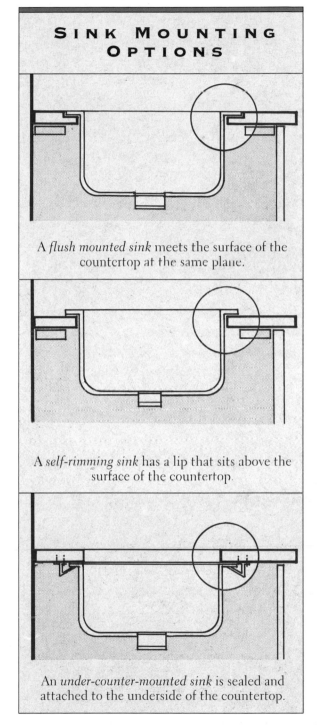

SINK MOUNTING OPTIONS

A *flush mounted sink* meets the surface of the countertop at the same plane.

A *self-rimming sink* has a lip that sits above the surface of the countertop.

An *under-counter-mounted sink* is sealed and attached to the underside of the countertop.

pan (a baking sheet, for example, or the roasting pan you need to wash in the bathtub every Thanksgiving) and make sure it fits, *flat*, in your proposed sink. Another piece of sound advice is to always buy a sink that is bigger than you think you need.

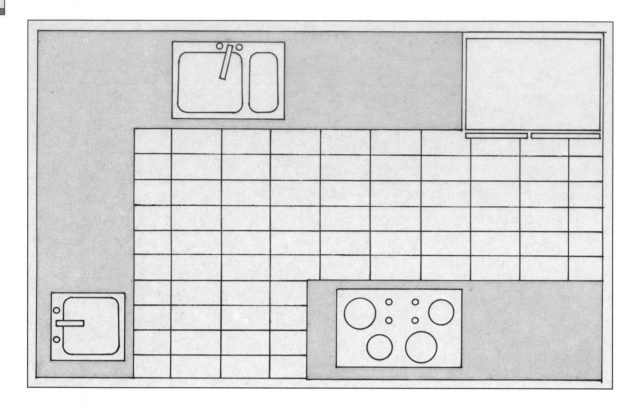

You might think, single sink is good, double sink is better, triple sink is best of all, but in fact, one good-sized bowl is generally more useful than two or three half-sized ones. A well-proportioned double sink, however, or a double sink with a small third bowl in the center for draining or compost collecting can be an excellent choice, provided that the large bowls are in fact large enough for pan washing.

Surprisingly, after looking at all of the kitchens researched for this book, I now believe that the most important thing about sinks is not what material or size they are, but that you have, if possible, two of them!

Second-best would be two sinks joined together in one spot, as in a double sink. But best of all would be an arrangement of two sinks of almost any reasonable size and conformation that are in two different places in your kitchen. (But don't let either of them be a bar sink—they are just too small to be useful for anything besides a water fountain.)

Two different sinks work because they allow you to separate the food-preparation sink from the kitchen clean-up sink. Thus a large-pan–sized sink would work very well near the dishwasher and clean-up wet area, while a smaller but still reasonably sized single, double, or even triple sink would make sense at a wet food-preparation area. This dividing of the WET zone into clean-up and preparation also gives you the possibility of locating one WET area near the refrigerator, for example, and another near the stove. Even if you choose one sink, a large, equally sized double bowl will enable you to designate one side of the sink for food prep and the other for clean-up.

Although sink shape and configuration are important, even more important is the height at which the sink is mounted and its depth. Sinks are quite often mounted too low, particularly for dishwashing purposes. Comfort at the kitchen clean-up sink can be greatly increased by slightly raising—by one or two inches—the counter in which that sink is mounted. Many people prefer to wash dishes sitting down on a kitchen stool. If this is the case in your household, the sink must be mounted with space for knees, either by eliminating the doors under the sink, or by eliminating any false drawer front so that full-size cabinet doors can be left open while dish washing is in progress. A storage space for the stool must also be planned.

When considering sinks of differing depths and conformations, think too about those that have little wire baskets and tubs that fit inside them. Large sinks with smaller inserts that temporarily subdivide the space as needed are extremely practical designs. If they fit in your budget, do consider them. And if they don't fit in your budget, look around at inexpensive plastic containers that will fit in your large sink—a small square dishpan can make a large sink much more practical for everyday dish or vegetable washing. It will also provide you with an easy way to collect "gray water" for use on house and garden plants, provided a biodegradable detergent is used.

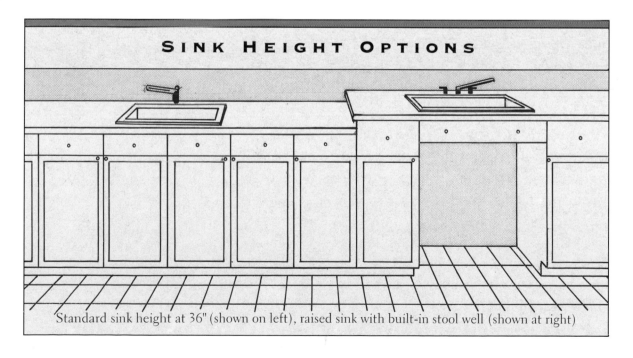

SINK HEIGHT OPTIONS

Standard sink height at 36" (shown on left), raised sink with built-in stool well (shown at right)

If you are creating a new kitchen on a tight budget, the sink is one place where you can sacrifice high style and expense with very little sacrifice in functionality. Inexpensive stainless-steel sinks (get the best quality you can afford) are available in every home center/hardware store in America, and they are extremely functional and durable. Two such large single sinks might be a more useful choice in the long run than one gorgeous designer object.

GARBAGE DISPOSAL UNITS

Garbage disposals grind up food wastes mixed with water and flush the resulting slurry into sewage lines. It is for this reason that ecologically minded cooks hold them in bad repute—what's the point of throwing all that good stuff in, grinding it up, and then not being able to use it for anything? Manufacturers have begun to respond to this good question by producing ecologically responsible products. For example, Carbco Industries has invented a Kich'n Komposter, which attaches to a disposal and spins dry the shredded material for manual retrieval to a composter. This can be an advantageous arrangement, because shredding allows the material to break down more rapidly in the soil and thus speeds up the process of composting.

Another alternative to a conventional garbage disposal is Waste Not's compost chute and bucket arrangement, which replaces existing garbage disposals with a hollow pipe leading to a compost-collecting bucket and is similarly designed for retrofitting purposes.

Until new garbage-disposal units are designed for composting, only you know if the convenience of such a unit outweighs its present irresponsible design.

TRASH COMPACTORS

Trash compactors use electrical energy to compress garbage into smaller masses. Like sink disposals, they make little sense to ecologically minded cooks, and as communities require separating different materials for recycling, they will begin to make less sense for everyone.

Hand-operated can smashers, however, do make sense for households where garbage is sorted for recycling and where large amounts of canned goods are used.

The truth is, trash compacters are a commercial response to overpackaging. If more foods were purchased in bulk in reusable or recyclable containers, much of the need for a compactor would disappear.

FAUCETS

If you have strict design priorities, along with the highest aesthetic standards and a large budget, you will be pleased by the variety of sink hardware available. In the "money is no object" category you will find such conveniences as faucets with long-

hosed retractable shower heads, instant boiling water attachments, and integral liquid soap dispensers. Hot and cold water controls can range in design from the minimalist to the bold. Some faucets are even made to be operated by an elbow or foot.

If you just want the water to emerge reliably from the faucet, however, a reasonable solution is to buy a midline faucet set at a home center. Many manufacturers produce faucet lines that are functional and dependable but limited in design and color choice.

Whatever your budget and your visual priorities, here is what you need to know in terms of materials and functions while "speaking faucet":

The best faucets are made of heavy solid brass, either left alone, plated with other metals, coated with epoxy color, or baked with an enameled finish. (Cheaper and less durable faucets are made of thinner metals with a brass wash.)

Check that the lacquer finish on the metal has been applied smoothly, and remember that, as with sinks, epoxy and enamel can fade or chip. Also keep in mind that although dark colors are not desirable if they show off toothpaste spatters in bathroom sinks, they can turn a kitchen sink into an attractive and dramatic focal point.

There are a surprising number of variations on how to turn the water on. In addi-

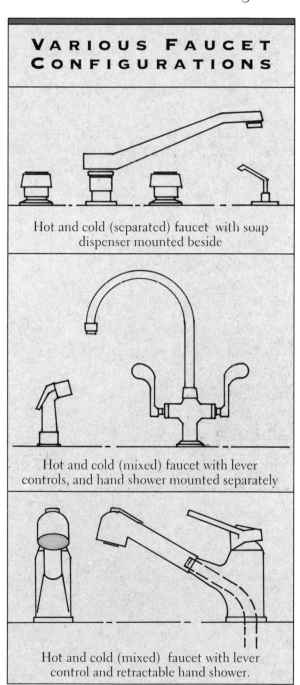

VARIOUS FAUCET CONFIGURATIONS

Hot and cold (separated) faucet with soap dispenser mounted beside

Hot and cold (mixed) faucet with lever controls, and hand shower mounted separately

Hot and cold (mixed) faucet with lever control and retractable hand shower.

tion to considering your own tastes when making a choice, you might want to consider the effect of an exotic faucet on your friends and family. We brought back a museum-quality kitchen faucet from Denmark that fits our exacting design and aesthetic standards and looks wonderful in our kitchen, but we have found that our guests are often at a loss as to how to make it work! We have incorporated basic faucet instruction into our usual "welcome to our house" tour in self-defense.

Basically, the choice is between separate hot and cold levers or faucets, and a single faucet (mixer) that (logically enough) mixes the two so that the water emerges in one stream. Although common American sink arrangements have included a separate spray wash attachment, an increasingly common upscale variation on this design is a faucet head that is itself retractable and encompasses a hand-shower attachment. The conveniences of such a gadget are many—from rinsing the dishes and sink to filling tall pots and other containers.

Faucets with lever controls seem to have a more sensitive adjustment for the *amount* of water that comes out than do faucets with handles—you can turn them on full for high pressure and maximum flow and put them on at intermediate points for less pressure and flow. Make sure that you try out any faucet handle you are considering; even with dry hands you will be able to detect the differences and choose one that feels comfortable to you.

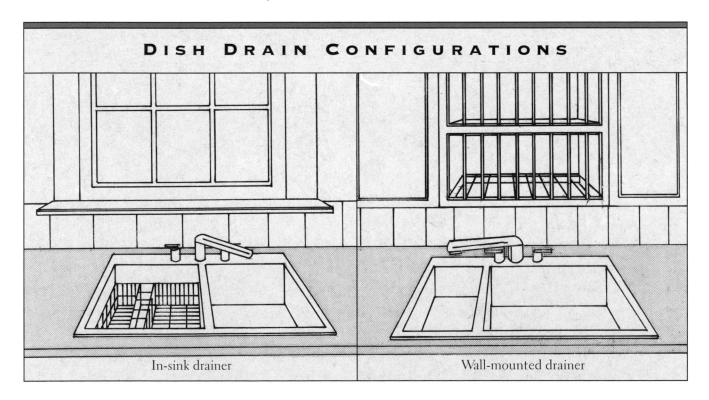

DISH DRAIN CONFIGURATIONS

In-sink drainer

Wall-mounted drainer

Not all faucets have to be operated with hands. Several of the cooks in the test kitchen of *Eating Well* magazine (who test a great many chicken recipes) suggested that home cooks might want to consider water systems that are operated by the elbow (as in surgical faucets) or foot. This seems a sound idea, eliminating the possibility of bacterial contamination from food to hand to faucet.

Keep in mind too, particularly if you are having a large sink custom-made, that the size, projection, and reach of the faucets should be matched to the size of the sink. Obviously, if the faucet isn't long enough, all washing will be done up against the faucet wall of the sink, leaving the rest of the area to be a dirty dish garage.

DISH DRAINERS

Although dishwashers are standard issue in most kitchens, there will always be some special items that need to be hand washed and allowed to drip dry. At least 18 inches of counterspace is necessary on one side of the sink (the opposite side from that used to store dirty dishes) to accommodate these items either on a folded dish towel or a standard dish drainer.

Consider a traditional wall-hung dish drainer—these can be made of wood, plastic-coated metal, or rigid plastic. They are often constructed of slatted wood and dowels to hold dishes on edge, but some are made of plastic and feature glass-drying storage areas as well. When located over a sink they need no additional drainage area, but when placed over a counter, they need to be provided with a removable drip pan. In Israel, most kitchens feature models that can be retracted into a bottomless standard overhead cabinet when not in use. Finnish drying cabinets are permanently set into overhead cupboards behind closed doors.

DISHWASHERS

There are many kinds of residential dishwashers available in a wide range of prices. One practical difference between low priced and high-priced models is in the amount (if any) of prewashing or rinsing that the dishes require before loading, and whether or not the machine uses the home's hot water system or heats its own water. Models that heat their own water are preferable, otherwise you waste energy keeping the whole house's hot water up to dishwasher temperature. Also, if you are concerned about sterilization, make sure that the dishwasher you are considering has such a setting or boosts the heat up to boiling.

Other factors to consider in choosing a dishwasher include the noise level, the amount of insulation, and the degree to which the interior is made of metal (more durable) or plastic. Remarkably, dishwashers sold at only slightly varying price points and manufactured by the same producer may vary enormously in sound level. If you are sensitive to noise, do try to listen to a machine in use before purchasing (ask your store if it can provide you with references) and consider looking for those that are rated quietest by consumer testing.

Finally, look closely at the internal configuration and accommodations for glassware, silver, and china. There are enormous variations in how dishwashers are loaded, and you will want to consider what will work best for you. Some models allow for varying arrangements depending on the load, with lift-up racks that can be reconfigured. Others save space by stacking silverware in a basket mounted on the inside of the door, allowing more room in the interior for larger pieces of china or glass.

Programming, too, can be a concern. If you have lower electric rates at off-peak hours, for example, it may be worth the additional money to have a dishwasher that you can program to go on in the late evening. (All residential dishwashers are now required to have a "no-heat dry" setting, to allow customers to save energy.)

In contrast, commercial dishwashers are designed to perform at high speed, often with four-minute cycles that include sterilization. However, commercial dishwashers do not have baskets or shelves that are configured for dinnerware, glassware, and silverware, making them much harder to load efficiently. They are also considerably more expensive to buy—and to operate, because they use more energy than residential models.

Along with a recommendation for considering two sinks, I would urge avid cooks and frequent entertainers (or those with large families) to consider two dishwashers. Having a dishwasher allocated to food-preparation cleanup and another designated for mealtime dishes allows the washing to be staggered and the contents stored near the areas they serve. As long as neither is run on less than a full load, there need not be any increase in energy use.

WET MATERIALS

Standing water rots wood. This is an important fact to keep in mind when planning materials to be set around WET places. A wooden counter, for example, or even an applied wooden bullnose edge set onto another countertop material will not stand up well to water near a sink, even if it is diligently coated with many layers of a marine varnish. The wood will eventually reveal the damage by discoloring, at the very least.

Similarly, although ceramic and marble tiles are nearly impervious to water, the cements used to attach them and the plywood that underlies them make both a less hardy choice of material for WET. What this means is that tiles set around sinks often become loose, particularly if water can stand on them or leak under them (as in a sink backsplash where water collects).

COUNTERTOPS

Most kitchen experts agree that the best countertops for WET places are unbroken expanses of laminates, such as Formica; solid surfacing, such as Corian; stone, such as marble or granite; or metal, such as stainless steel. It makes sense to have the right countertop material for the job at hand, and the variety of appropriate WET possibilities is large enough so that visually pleasing surfaces can be mixed within a kitchen.

Of these choices, plastic laminates known by brand names such as Formica or Wilsonart are the least expensive. They are offered with various edge details. The least expensive configuration, postformed, is an integrated backsplash, counter, and edge. This alternative works well for straight runs of counter in standard distances, but it has to be mitered (joined with an angled cut) or butt-joined (joined straight

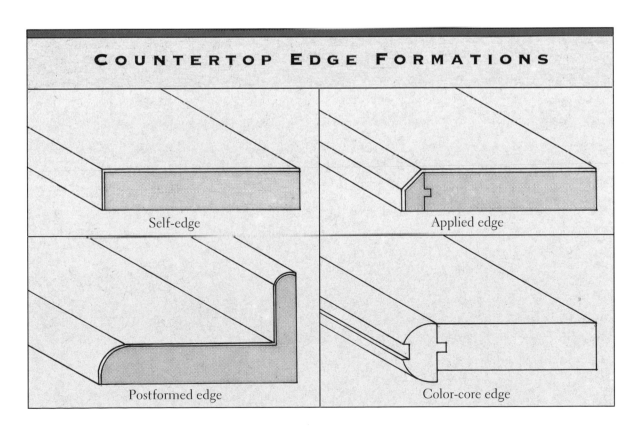

COUNTERTOP EDGE FORMATIONS

Self-edge

Applied edge

Postformed edge

Color-core edge

edge to straight edge) at corners. It has a distinctive look, as the edge where the counter meets the backsplash is curved, as is the front plane. Lovers of things retro find the look of postformed counters perfect for recreating that fifties ambiance. Some choose it for sound financial reasons, preferring to free the budget for more important items.

Other laminate-edge possibilities include self-edge (where the same laminate is glued on to the front edge of the countertop, leaving a thin black line at the joints) and applied edge details, such as a hardwood strip that can be shaped in various configurations (a bullnose is one example).

Another possibility is color-through laminate, which is considerably more expensive. The use of these laminates eliminates the thin black edging line and creates a more solid look. The edge of color-through laminate can also be decoratively shaped on a router, creating a custom visual signature.

Because laminate sheets are manufactured in 12-foot lengths, most countertops that are made entirely of laminate end up with seams. These seams, unfortunately, create opportunities for water to penetrate and degrade the wood understructure of the laminate. This is a very good argument for making countertops of different materials at different stations in the kitchen. For example, a solid unseamed laminate area could have a sink cut out of its center. The water-vulnerable seams could be stationed some distance from the sink, at which point the countertop material could change to something more appropriate—a heat-resistant material for the HOT zone, for example (next to the stove), or a cool material for a COLD area (such as marble in a pastry counter).

When considering laminates, bear in mind that a matte finish always wears better than a gloss one, and that lighter colors are easier to keep clean. Do not allow yourself to be persuaded that a "dirt-colored" (brown or gray) counter will show less dirt. First of all, it won't, as dirt comes in many colors, but further, remember that this is your kitchen, where you want to be able to see the dirt so that you can get rid of it! Cooking demands a clean environment, and if you can't see soil clearly, you won't necessarily think to clean it.

Another countertop material that performs excellently under WET conditions is solid surfacing, usually known under its brand names of Corian, Avonite, Fountainhead by Nevamar, Surell, and Gibraltar. This strong integral material can be repaired or reconfigured by filling and patching, sanding, or cutting. It is expensive, but it comes with a number of advantages: First, it is stable and resistant to fading and warping. Some manufacturers (Wilsonart, for instance) match their colors of solid surfacing to their line of laminate, making it possible to blend both materials unobtrusively, as in a laminate counter with a solid surfaced edge. This provides the appearance of solid surfacing at a substantially reduced cost. Similarly, other manufacturers (DuPont, for example) sell sinks of solid surface materials with matching colors that can be undermounted and bonded to the countertop, producing a virtually seamless installation. Note that solid surfacing must be installed by a certified fabricator in order to qualify for guarantees against manufacturing defects. Note too that allergy-prone and environmentally sensitive people may have difficulty in tolerating the emissions from the glues in plywood, particle board, and the glue used to attach laminates to those underlays.

Even more expensive and durable are stone surfaces, such as custom-cut slate, marble, and granite, with slate being the least expensive and granite the costliest. Stone countertops actually need not be the most expensive solution: An acquaintance's kitchen has beautiful black slate counters made of the back, more textured side of discarded black slate school blackboards. They are edged in natural wood, and although she has to be scrupulous about keeping water off the edge, the counter is gorgeous, impervious to heat, and dramatic. Another inexpensive possibility is to buy marble off-cuts, or surplus cuts, or even partially cut slabs directly from the quarry. Many Vermonters and visitors to the state have marble countertop areas in their kitchens, thanks to the availability at low cost of this local material. It is also possible to use stone tiles in place of solid stone for a similar appearance at substantially lower cost. Stone tiles have the same disadvantages as ceramic tiles, however, in that the grout has to be maintained and guarded against water damage.

Counters of solid custom-cut stone are indeed a high-ticket item, but increasingly many people feel that the advantages of this material outweigh its expense. Naturally, it is extremely durable around WET areas, although the hardness of the material makes breakage inevitable, should dishes or glassware slip. Remember, too, that making the cut-out for the sink is going to be a high-risk and therefore expensive proposition. Some advise going to the quarry to choose the particular stone you want, to guard against discrepancies between the look of a small sample and that of a larger piece. The most expensive granite or stone counters have rounded and decoratively cut edge details that considerably add to the total cost. Straight-edged stone counters, because they are easier to cut, are actually nearly comparable in price to solid surfacing.

Criticisms of these materials are based both on looks and on wearing power. Slate is usually dark, which makes spots show up dramatically; marble is a porous stone, and high-gloss finishes will permanently record any lemon juice or oil spilled on them; granite's sheen provides a perfect backdrop for fingerprints, which need to be removed frequently with window cleaner. But stone, like laminates and solid surfacing, makes an excellent surface for WET.

Finally, stainless steel is such an excellent WET material, because it is impervious to water damage and is easy to clean, that most commercial kitchens use it exclusively in WET areas. Commercial sinks are often fabricated with integral drainboards to exploit the useful properties of the material. It is, however, extremely sound-conducting, so that kitchens with stainless-steel counters tend to be noisy. And as with sinks made of this material, drying or polishing may be required with some regularity.

As you are thinking about the sink area, note that standard backsplashes are 4 inches high, and if made of laminate they are usually ¾ inch thick. Many kitchens would profit from higher backsplashes, which can ease cleaning splatters, protect wall surfaces, and provide decorative opportunities for color and pattern.

RECYCLING
AND COLLECTING

Now that many localities require people to separate their garbage, more and more kitchens resemble mini–recycling centers. Large kitchens can accommodate built-in bins and cabinets designed specifically to hide recyclables. A recycling center built specifically for that purpose can be constructed of the same cabinetry as the rest of the kitchen and can be provided with a shelf for newspapers and provision behind closed doors for a rolling trolley (many are on the market) that contains bins for aluminum, clear and colored glasses, and plastics.

People with smaller kitchens can sort and tie bundles on the kitchen table and store recyclables in a closet or garage. As recycling becomes more widespread, more and more manufacturers are creating products designed to aid the sorting and storage process. On the market today are a variety of plastic, cardboard, wood, canvas, and wire arrangements. There is no easy solution, but for recycling to work, we have to find ways to make it convenient.

COMPOST

It has been calculated that each American deposits 3½ pounds of trash daily, and that 15 to 20 percent of that waste is from food, which can easily be returned to enrich the earth through a process called composting. Composting is actually controlled rotting, which is accomplished aerobically (with air), or anaerobically (without the presence of air). Anyone can compost in very little space and with a minimum expenditure of time, effort, and money. Composting is one activity that nearly everyone can do that will have an immediate and appreciable effect on the earth.

COMPOST COLLECTING SITES

The composting process starts with the collection of suitable material into a holding bucket. In the kitchen, materials for compost include peelings from food preparation, leftovers from plates, and biodegradable paper, such as paper towels. In the garden, suitable materials for compost include grass clippings, crumbled leaves, weeds, dead plants, and the leavings from the vegetable garden, such as cornstalks and pea vines.

Retrofitting an old kitchen to accommodate new requirements for compost collecting does not have to be difficult. The collection site should be located near the sink in the WET zone, so that you can dump and rinse in one smooth motion. There are a number of possible solutions to the storage problem, depending on your preferences. One possibility is to make a new cutout with a flush-mounted cover set in a countertop, so that the bucket can be stored, open, in the cabinet below

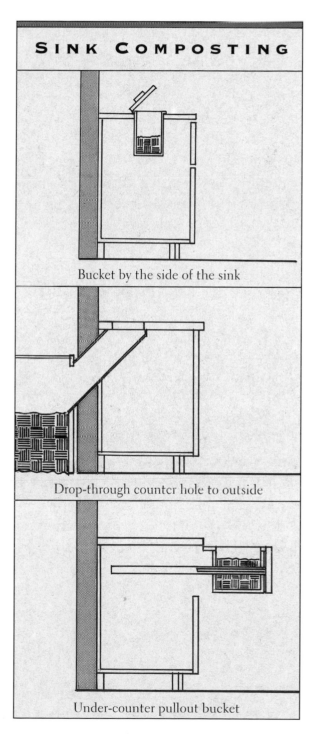

SINK COMPOSTING

Bucket by the side of the sink

Drop-through counter hole to outside

Under-counter pullout bucket

for easy retrieval. This could be located to the right or left of the cleanup or the food-prep sink, depending on the rest of your traffic pattern. Another possibility is a pull-out under a sink or adjacent cabinet, or a foot-pedal arrangement on the floor. (A number of manufacturers sell appropriate designs for collection of compost and sorted trash. See Sources for more information.) These solutions are relatively easy retrofits and can be accommodated in most kitchens with only minor reorganization.

When you are planning a new kitchen, it makes good sense to consider compost collecting at the start, as an integral part of meal cleanup. An excellent idea from David Goldbeck, author of *The Smart Kitchen*, is a drop-through hole to a garbage can in an exterior wall section of the kitchen counter to collect food wastes. The can would be accessible only through a well-insulated exterior door, to be carried directly to the compost pile. Similarly, an inexpensive chute could be constructed out of smooth pipe or sheet metal that would connect a kitchen deposit point in a counter, wall chute, or cabinet to a collection pail in the basement or an outdoor attached shed.

Other specifically designed solutions are now on the market, and we can expect more of them as composting becomes more common. For example, Blanco of Germany manufactures a sink with a built-in waste chute that deposits waste into a bucket located beneath the sink for compost purposes.

COMPOSTING METHODS

Collecting the materials for compost constitutes one step; actually composting the materials is another. There are many composting methods, both high-tech and low-tech. High-tech methods include closed collecting bins with mechanical parts designed to shift and aerate the mass (compost tumblers), and Green Cones, designed solely for kitchen waste, which are partially buried and drain into the earth. Low-tech methods include dumping the compost materials outdoors into wire or cement block bins, layering alternately wet and dry materials, and allowing them to decompose over time. Some of these devices are listed in the Sources section, and books that include compost information are listed on pages 150–151.

Apartment dwellers without back yards could perhaps consider those small tumbler models that claim to produce composted soil in weeks without odor, or a Green Cone placed in a pan of cat litter on a fire escape, which could produce workable compost in short order as well. (Even without land to grow crops on, you will have thriving houseplants. Or you can donate either the raw materials of compost or finished bags of rich soil to your neighborhood park or community garden.)

In New York City, the rooftop of the Cathedral of St. John the Divine now supports an experimental organic garden site using raised beds enriched with compost. Gardeners there project that if all usable roof sites in New York were planted this way they could raise all of the city's food. This would make urban compost more than another "black gold"—it could even create a profitable cottage industry.

Remember, no matter what method you use to compost, it significantly reduces landfill waste crowding, and it enriches the earth that we are so rapidly depleting.

COMPOSTING WITH WORMS

■■■

Remarkably, there are now one-step composters on the market that are actual worm farms—a ventilated drawer near the sink, filled with moistened sawdust or shredded newspaper and a good "red wiggler" worm population. Kitchen scraps are fed directly into the drawer, where the resident population goes to work on them! In short order, good rich black earth can be harvested. If you are interested in buying or constructing such accommodations for these working guests, see Sources for an address.

Those who are uneasy about worms in the house could move the worm site to another location—a basement, perhaps—provided that the temperature in the new worm domicile does not fall below 40 degrees. A chute that carries food waste to a worm box in the basement would avoid too close a relationship between the worms and their human hosts.

DRY ZONE

WHAT SOME KITCHEN PLANNERS CALL DRY PREPARATION (OR MOSTLY dry—some liquids are often added) is commonly known as food preparation. It is the process of assembling raw ingredients into finished meals, and it is this sequence of activities that will require the major runs between counter, cabinet, and storage space in your kitchen.

These activities include chopping and mixing food by hand or by machine (cutting boards, electrical stations for WET zone/DRY zone overlaps, such as the blender, food processor, mixer); arranging food (plating area, serving-platter storage); and baking prep—pastry mixing, blending, kneading, shaping (this pastry area can be combined with DRY, as it is here, or can be thought of as COLD).

Because DRY interacts with WET (as in adding liquids to dishes, as well as cleanup), the two should be located in adjacent areas. (Many of the small electrical appliances mentioned in the WET zone section on storage are used in the DRY zone as well.)

It is very useful to be on a direct line with the refrigerator for transporting the raw materials to the food-preparation area, and it is useful to have dry-food storage also located nearby, or easily accessible. Most frequently, DRY is located along a long run of counter that lies either adjacent to the sink, perpendicular to the sink, or opposite it, as in an island. At the opposite side from WET, DRY most often merges into HOT, with the stove or cooktop marking another nearby boundary.

DRY FOOD STORAGE

Where should you keep the food that doesn't need refrigeration? Traditional locales (discussed more fully on page 36) are pantries, larders, and root cellars; their modern counterparts are open-shelf storage, "pantry" cupboards, built-in bins, and ventilated drawers and baskets within cupboards. It makes sense to have the ingredients you need as close as possible to where you use them.

DRY storage means finding places for staples like canned goods, condiments, oils and vinegars, crackers, flours and sugars, cereals, dried legumes, pastas, teas and

FOOD STORAGE PLANNING OPTIONS

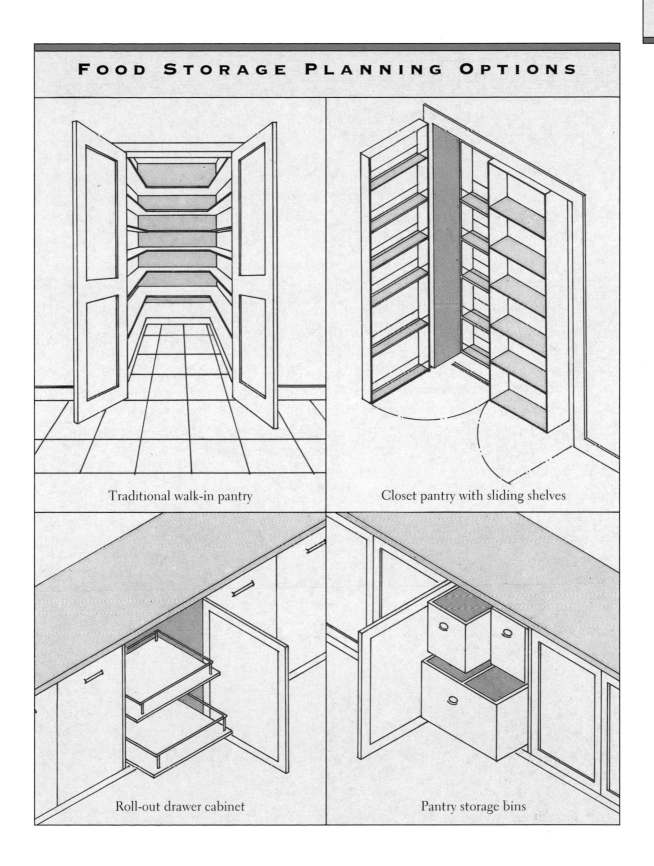

Traditional walk-in pantry

Closet pantry with sliding shelves

Roll-out drawer cabinet

Pantry storage bins

coffees, packets of powdered milk, instant soups, and unopened bottled sauces; as well as paper goods, pet foods, bottles, and canned beverages. In many homes, once-opened food that has been purchased in cardboard containers or paper bags will need to be repackaged and stored in airtight bug- and rodent-proof containers.

Nonrefrigerated storage space is also required for perishables like fruits and breads. In regions of the world where refrigerators are much smaller—most of Europe, for example—much of what Americans store in refrigerators is stored instead in cool rooms or closets called larders. Butter, eggs, cakes, and many vegetables rest in baskets on shelves, and breads are kept in bread boxes, tins, or covered clay crocks. Keep in mind, however, that in these regions kitchens are generally kept cooler, and because daily shopping is a tradition, most food stored is consumed almost immediately.

MODERN PANTRY LOCALES

Sites for closed pantry storage are ventilated drawers in undercabinets, open-out pantry cupboards, shelves in cabinets, and wall-mounted storage systems. Open storage can be on shelves in a kitchen or storeroom. Wreaths of chilies, ropes of garlic, and inverted bunches of herbs can be hung in garlands along walls or pantry shelves. When the pantry is somewhat removed from the center of the kitchen, baskets, a rolling cart, or trays may be used for transport purposes (they will need to be stored when out of use).

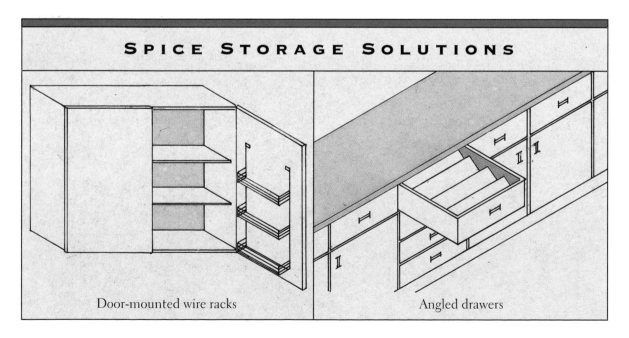

SPICE STORAGE SOLUTIONS

Door-mounted wire racks   Angled drawers

STORING DRY FOOD: CONTAINERS

■ ■ ■

It is visually satisfying to have food stored in containers that are like each other, whether in size or material. Glass is a particularly attractive material for dry food storage because the contrasting textures and colors of grains, beans, flours, cereals, and rice look alluring side by side.

There are many ways to amass a suitable storage-jar collection: New glass canning jars in pints, quarts, and half-gallons are available quite reasonably by the case in rural community feed stores, supermarkets, and food co-ops. Beautiful antique canning jars, often tinted blue and with glass tops or with metal screw caps, can still be found at low prices at yard sales and flea markets. Cooks who buy the same new products consistently can amass a matched set of containers by washing and saving the jars, whether they are attractive small jam jars or giant institutional-size mayonnaise jars (which can sometimes be gotten by asking deli departments for their empties). Very beautiful new glass jars are available at retail, such as fluted green glass cork-topped containers from Italy and Spain, or austere French and Finnish glass canning jars with vacuum seals and wire clasps.

Finally, when you are thinking about DRY food storage, a place for frequently used spices needs to be planned. Ideally, dried herbs and spices should be stored near the stove but out of range of heat and light. A useful idea from *Eating Well* magazine's test kitchen is to arrange spices alphabetically by cuisine in special angled drawers. Cooks who grind their own spices or create spice blends will want to make additional storage provision for a spice grinder and/or a mortar and pestle.

TOOLS AND EQUIPMENT (BATTERIE DE CUISINE)

Serious cooks tend to collect serious equipment, from massive stockpots and copper saucepans to pasta machines, pizza stones, juicers, and ice cream makers. Where to put it all? Restaurant kitchens can show us the functional beauty of frequently used

KNIVES

###

Good sharp knives make all the difference in ease of preparation and in safety, because you are more apt to cut yourself with a dull knife than with one that is consistently kept honed.

Until the middle of this century, the best knives were made of carbon steel, which, although it held a fine edge well and had a good weight, discolored and corroded in response to acidic foods. New advances in metals have led to knives made entirely of stainless steel, which are difficult to get sharp and keep sharp, and a hybrid: high-carbon stainless steel, which is now considered by some to be the best material for blades.

All knives are either stamped or forged. Stamped blades are thinner, about 20 percent lighter, and less expensive than forged. They require more effort on the part of the cook, because their lightness forces the hand to exert more pressure. Forged knives require a more complex and careful manufacturing process, which results in a finished knife that is better balanced and weighted toward the front of the blade.

All knives have tangs, a rear extension of the blade, to which the handle is attached. The best knives have tangs that run the full length of the knife. Less expensive knives have partial tangs.

A very basic knife collection would include one each of the following:

CHEF'S KNIFE: A large, broad bladed knife (usually 10 inches but available in a wide range of lengths from 6 inches up to 12 or 14 inches, depending on the manufacturer). This is a true all-purpose knife, and one that few kitchens could be without for slicing, chopping, and even carving.

PARING KNIFE: Available in an enormous variety of styles, from spearpoint to bird's beak to sheep's foot and beyond. A paring knife is a small (3½- to 4-inch) knife that is used for peeling, fine chopping, piercing, and slicing.

BONING KNIFE: Less than useful for vegetarian kitchens but essential for all others, this thin and flexible knife makes boning meat easy. It can also be used for very thin slicing.

BREAD KNIFE: A serrated (wavy-edge) knife is essential for cutting bread. The heavier the blade and the sharper the edge, the easier it will be to cut thinly and well. A serrated knife is also useful for cutting cakes and can be used, in a pinch, to cut frozen food.

cookware hanging close at hand, and the rest stacked on open stainless steel wire shelves. Whatever your solution, whether open to view or behind closed doors, accessible storage for these items must be allowed for in your kitchen planning.

Smaller food-preparation tools include measuring cups, spoons, scales, mixing bowls, rolling pins, cookie cutters, pastry bags and other decorating tools, baking sheets and pans, knives, and a knife sharpener. There are many solutions for these small-tool storage needs: open shelves, pegboards, storage drawers, tray cabinets (for baking sheets), baskets dedicated to cookie cutters, and so forth.

An avid baker might dedicate a drawer entirely to tools for pastry making—storing rolling pins, measuring cups and spoons, pastry bags and tips, cookie cutters, pastry brushes, parchment paper, and dough scrapers together for ease of use. This could be located next to a deep vertical tray cabinet for baking sheets and pans.

Parents who do a lot of baking with children might find it useful to maintain a separate area for small-scale tools. We have a box that holds small rolling pins, cookie cutters, a miniature pasta machine, small bowls, colanders, and spatulas. When one of the children wants to cook, it is a simple matter for her to bring the whole box from its out-of-the-way cupboard home to the counter to find the tools that fit her hand best.

Specialized ethnic cooks might find it useful to create cabinets for each cuisine's tools and equipment, such as a storage area that holds woks of various sizes, bamboo steamers, mesh strainers, cooking chopsticks, spoons, and spatulas. In such a kitchen, the cook might also want to store the spices and condiments for that cuisine near its tools, if that is a practical solution for his or her space needs.

The point of any efficient storage scheme is to enable cooks to find what they need easily. How you classify and organize your equipment will reflect your particular style, habits, and needs. The important thing is remembering to consider them in advance of space planning.

To aid efficient storage, many European kitchen cabinet manufacturers, and now American high-end cabinet companies, produce interior fittings for base cabinets that are designed for specialized storage and use needs. These include Ikea's Rationell system, Elfa's line of wrapped wire fittings (both of which can be retrofitted into existing cabinets), and Smallbone's basket and ventilated drawers (available only with the purchase of their furniture), as well as numerous American options produced by kitchen cabinet manufacturers as well as by manufacturers of specialized hardware.

STORING KNIVES

■■■

Knives must be stored safely, to protect both their blades and the hands of cooks. Countertop knife blocks are one solution, and built-in knife slots in drawers or recessed into counters are another, as are wall-hung (often magnetic) units. Whichever solution you choose, make sure that knives are stored securely and away from children's reach. Fine knives should be hand-washed and dried carefully before being put away.

DRY MATERIALS

Countertops for DRY areas can usefully be constructed out of many diverse materials, so it makes sense to think about the different kinds of food preparation that take place here. For example, every DRY preparation area will need a place to cut bread and chop vegetables: either a pullout (or take-out) cutting board, a cutting board recessed into a countertop of another material, or a butcher-block countertop area. Separate (and replaceable) cutting boards should be reserved for poultry and meats. (Recent research indicates, surprisingly, that salmonella bacteria can persist on plastic boards, even after washing, but die within ten minutes on wooden boards.)

Pastry-making and bread-kneading operations profit from as smooth (and cold) surface as possible, such as stone or solid surfacing.

Mixing, blending, stirring, and folding can be messy; spills are most rapidly cleaned up on an easy-to-wipe surface such as laminate or stainless steel.

Finally, as DRY often functions as a preparation area for foods en route to HOT, as well as a plating area for foods on the way to the table, remember to plan the space accordingly, possibly incorporating a heat-safe surface on which to rest hot pots while spooning their contents onto serving dishes.

H O T   Z O N E

THE HOT PREPARATION ZONE IS THE SITE WHERE FOODSTUFFS ARE transformed through the use of heat. A wide variety of equipment can be involved, including stovetop burners (electric or gas), ovens, grills and griddles, broilers, and microwave ovens, as well as countertop convection ovens, toasters, and toaster ovens.

Each of these pieces of equipment, large and small, needs to have a space planned for it, whether it is permanently installed (a stove) or in temporary and mobile use (portable electric griddle, plug-in electric wok, slow cooker, or bread machine).

You will need to plan for special seasonal cooking activities, such as space for canning jars and a water-bath canning kettle, as well as a pressure canner, if used.

And further, each of these pieces of equipment has ancillary equipment that needs storage as well—stovetop and oven require many of the large and bulky items mentioned in DRY zone storage, such as pots and pans, baking dishes, baking sheets, cooling racks, and casseroles. The stove area should also include a place nearby for hand tools, such as mixing spoons, pastry brushes, carving forks and knives, whisks, measuring cups, mixing bowls, and wooden, metal, and rubber spatulas.

The microwave has spawned a whole other set of ceramic, glass, or microwave-safe plastic pots and pans to cook in, and they also need storage, preferably near both the microwave and a HOT/DRY preparation area.

Aluminum foil is often a grilling aid; paper plates, plastic wrap, wax paper, and paper towels are used in the microwave. A drawer or wall-mounted arrangement for storing these items should be part of the plan.

Finishing tools for hot preparation can include strainers, steamers, and colanders in various sizes and materials, all of which demand storage space.

Protection from heat adds further storage requirements—hot pads, trivets, and pot holders all need to be close at hand without adding clutter and confusion.

HOT EQUIPMENT

HOT equipment comes in such a variety of forms and styles, it can easily be the most difficult series of decisions to make in planning a new kitchen. Cooktop and oven(s) or one-piece range? Residential manufacturer or commercial? Gas, electric, or a combination of both? A built-in microwave or a freestanding model on a countertop? Separate grill (downdraft countertop? commercial freestanding? built-in griddle as part of a stovetop?) Restaurant salamander? A broiler that is part of the oven? How many ovens, and of what type—wall or under stovetop? Single or double? And what about solid-fuel cookers (like an Aga), or wood-fired baking ovens or brick pizza ovens? Or a restaurant wok? Finally, should a fireplace (and perhaps a Tuscan Grill to create all-year-round barbecues) have a place in your new kitchen? Would a small cast-iron woodstove for heat and cooking complete your dream?

ONE-PIECE COOKSTOVES/RANGES

These freestanding stoves are efficient machines that have cooking surfaces, ovens, and (in residential and crossover models) an integral broiler. Some residential, crossover, and commercial models have optional griddles or grills on the stovetop surface. Because it concentrates all these different HOT functions into one space, a freestanding range is extremely useful. In small kitchens it focuses all HOT activity into one contained area, and in large kitchens it provides an anchor for HOT while allowing additional HOT stations (such as extra built-in wall ovens, or an additional set of burners or grill) to be placed elsewhere in the room.

In addition to space advantages, a range is also a good investment, as buying a whole is cheaper than buying parts.

COMMERCIAL RANGES

Strictly commercial ranges are offered by Garland, Vulcan, Wolf, and others. They are made for intense use, since in restaurants the burners and ovens are often on continuously. Heavy, deep, and poorly insulated, they demand both side and rear clearances from combustible surfaces, as well as an extensive exhaust system. For homeowners, their other drawbacks include an energy-wasting pilot light on cooktop and oven and the lack of a built-in broiler or self-cleaning features.

But these powerful stoves can nevertheless be wonderful workhorses when installed and used appropriately. Their extremely powerful burners make searing easy, and large burners allow big pots to cook efficiently. Large ovens provide ample

INTEGRAL COOKTOP/OVEN

Cooktop and oven as an integral unit in the kitchen

space for roasting huge turkeys, or baking four dozen cookies at a time.

Note that if you have your heart set on commercial equipment, it is often possible to buy at considerable savings extremely serviceable used stoves from restaurant equipment resale dealers or directly from restaurants that have gone out of business. These stoves can be acid-cleaned, resurfaced, and made almost new again for a fraction of their original price.

LUXURY COMMERCIAL/RESIDENTIAL HYBRIDS

Responding to the drawbacks of commercial ranges, many producers are now manufacturing crossover ranges that combine the appearance and some of the benefits of a commercial range with some of the advantages of residential models. Five Star and Viking, for example, sell restaurant-quality ranges in standard residential sizes. Made of stainless or enameled steel, they have sufficient insulation to sit flush with walls and standard-depth cabinets. They are built with energy-saving pilotless ignition; lights, windows, and optional continuous cleaning in the oven; and a broiler compartment. Aimed directly at the serious home cook, these scaled-down luxury models offer a choice of enameled colors and have either legs that correspond to the height of standard cabinet toe space (Five Star) or standard and custom curb bases (Viking).

MIDDLE-RANGE HYBRIDS

Striking a middle ground more toward the commercial, Wolf and Garland have created a black enamel or stainless-steel residential-use line that does not compromise on size or burner power, and like the examples above, has zero-clearance approval for home installations. Along with the now-standard crossover electric pilotless ignition, they offer such possibilities as a choice of a high-capacity electric broiler in the oven or a separate gas broiler under the griddle, conventional or convection baking, and a commercial-style highback with shelf. One model (by Wolf) even has two ovens in two sizes—one that is standard large-capacity commercial size and one that is scaled for fuel-efficient cooking of smaller amounts. The downside for design-conscious cooks, however, is that these stoves lack the sleek styling and clean lines of some of the newer crossover players.

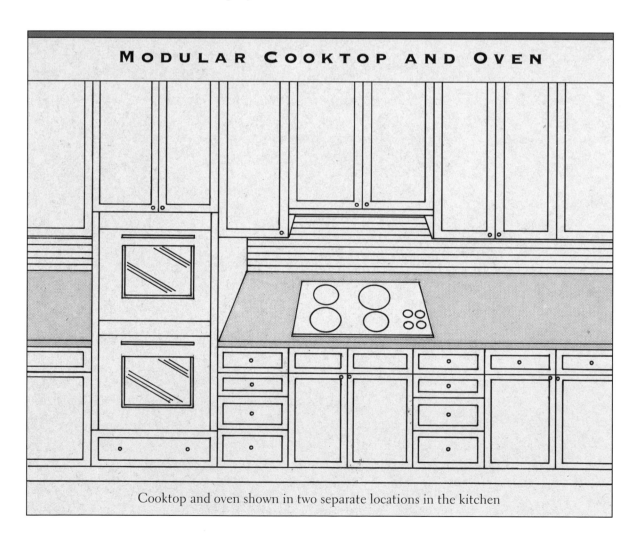

MODULAR COOKTOP AND OVEN

Cooktop and oven shown in two separate locations in the kitchen

ELECTRIC/GAS MODELS

It used to be that if you wished to cook on gas and bake with electric power, you had to buy separate components. This is no longer true, thanks to manufacturers who started paying attention to what people wanted. Now such brands as Jenn-Air and Thermador offer ranges with gas stovetops and electric ovens that switch from conventional to convection. Thermador's model provides an additional small warming or proofing oven.

MODULAR COOKTOPS

If your requirements are different from the standard—by reason of height, space, depth dimensions, or design—you may be better served by buying a separate stovetop component. In addition to the benefit of having this HOT element installed at a height and location that suit you best, your design choices—configuration, style, color, and surface material—will be greatly expanded.

The greatest advantage of modular cooktops for kitchens used by multiple cooks is that they allow you to create more than one cooking station. Cooktops come in a variety of configurations, with staggered burners or burners in parallel lines. Each of these has its advantages. Staggered burners allow you to reach to the pots at the rear without much difficulty, while parallel burners make it easier to slide heavy pots around. It is also possible to have a choice of the number of burners, from two to four to six, which can be "ganged" to create a custom arrangement.

Surfaces with a continuous plane—like electric flat-glass induction, concealed-coil, and radiant-heat electric cooktops, or gas-fired commercial-style cast iron that runs edge to edge—allow pots to slide to any point on the stovetop and give cooks a versatile relationship to the actual heat source, in that pots can be placed to one side of a burner for gentle cooking.

When evaluating cooktops, notice the placement of controls. Those at the rear may provide an edge of child safety, but that benefit may be undercut by the additional risk of burn to an adult reaching over a heat source to turn the controls on and off. Experts generally agree that controls to one side or to the front are best.

Some cooktops have features that offer increased flexibility. Frigidaire's Euroflair, for example, allows you to mix both gas and electric elements in one stovetop surface. Others permit switching modules, so that one day you have a griddle and another day a grill. Still others make it possible to have a downdraft exhaust system on residential electric and gas models.

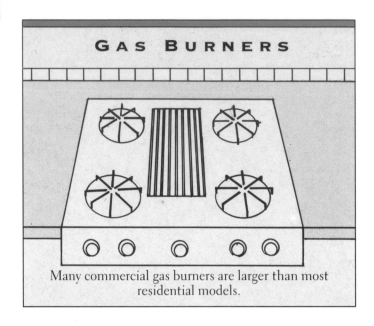

GAS BURNERS

Many commercial gas burners are larger than most residential models.

GAS COOKTOPS

Most serious cooks prefer cooking with gas, as they feel it provides more control over the heat source than electrical power. Each brand of commercial, crossover, and residential cooktops offers different advantages. For example, Russell Range's crossover commercially powered cooktop has a "safe-slide" grate system for ease in moving pots, as well as a wok ring. Their cooktops also fit flush alongside standard-depth cabinets and can be finished with a bullnose edge detail. Five Star's commercially inspired cooktops have a burner with the ability to maintain a very low simmer, and come in two sizes with optional trim kits for island installations. Wolf, long a name in commercial stoves, now produces cooktops with an infrared charbroiler that have the same "slide-in" ease of installation as conventional cooktops.

On the residential side, upscale manufacturers are now producing models that offer similar flexibility and burner strength: Gaggenau offers fast and normal burner choices, as well as configurative options, while Dacor offers surface ventilation along with variable BTU burners and multiple burner options.

ELECTRIC COOKTOPS

Similarly, with electrically powered cooktops, the choices are dizzying. Dacor, for example, makes a convertible cooktop that allows a user to choose between conventional coil, halogen, solid elements, a smooth glass-ceramic-topped (Ceran™) cooking surface, wok/canning large-burner options, and a griddle, barbecue, or rotisserie. For further choice, Dacor also sells a smooth glass-ceramic top, while Gaggenau manufactures an extra-large glass-ceramic-topped cooking surface powered by halogen.

All of these choices have implications for the pots and pans you use, your style of cooking, and the amount of energy that is consumed in the process.

Induction cooking features induction elements hidden beneath a glass-ceramic surface (Ceran) that generate an electromagnetic field that cooks food in magnetic-sensitive containers such as cast iron or steel. The advantage is that the cooktop stays cool, since it is not affected by the electromagnetic field, and (also unlike old-style electric burners) the cooking process starts and stops instantly with precise heat control.

Halogen cooking also provides sensitive temperature control under a glass surface, but the heat is generated from the gas in the halogen bulb. It can be used with any heat-safe pot, but it is currently an expensive option.

Radiant-heat cooking utilizes electric resistance coils beneath a glass surface. The burners do not start up or cool down as rapidly as halogen. Another kind of radiant-heat cooking uses solid disk or hobs, which are cast-iron or ceramic disks with heating elements under them. They heat up slowly and hold their heat for a long time, so that slow simmering is possible after they have been turned off.

Because each option has advantages and disadvantages, many manufacturers offer cooktops that combine various elements.

MODULAR BUILT-IN RADIANT OVENS

Modular ovens have the same advantages as modular cooktops: flexibility in design. Powered by electricity or gas (many bakers feel that electric ovens produce the most even heat), they come in several sizes (standard oven interior dimensions can range from 27 to 36 inches wide, depending on brand and model) and in standard residen-

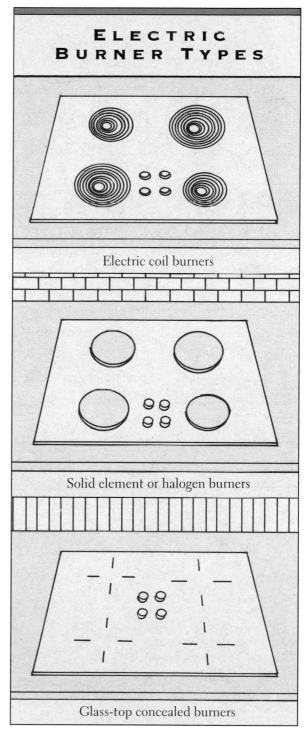

ELECTRIC BURNER TYPES

Electric coil burners

Solid element or halogen burners

Glass-top concealed burners

tial, crossover, or commercial models. Options can include self-cleaning settings, programmability (very helpful for setting the cooking to begin hours before you'll get home), an integral broiler, rotisserie, see-through glass door, interior lights, conventional or convection (circulating hot-air baking) cooking choices, and optional numbers of racks each oven can accommodate (with convection cooking, food will cook evenly when on many racks, because the circulating air promotes more even cooking). These ovens are available in single or double configurations. Most manufacturers produce double oven models that are configured vertically, which can mean that one oven is too high and the other too low. Cooks who are taller or shorter than average may prefer to buy two separate ovens and locate them appropriately for themselves.

MICROWAVE OVENS

Microwave ovens range in size from the miniature to full-sized, with options for the amount of power and for built-in or freestanding countertop models. Most cooks who microwave suggest that higher (over 600 watts) wattages are best, and that large microwaves are more useful than smaller ones. As in locating a conventional oven, keeping safety in mind is important in finding the right height for a microwave. Ideally, a microwave should be located between countertop and chest height, so that the contents can be removed with little risk of burning.

Because I am troubled by the possible health hazards posed by extra-low-frequency (ELF) electromagnetic radiation emitted by the microwave, I have located ours in the pantry, so that no one is near it when it is on. (All electrical appliances emit some ELF radiation. We make it a practice to keep our distance from the toaster when it is on as well. ELF radiation drops off dramatically at 3 feet.)

SPECIALIZED COOKERS

Many ambitious home cooks find that they want to duplicate the flavors of foods eaten while traveling abroad or at certain restaurants at home. Many, too, have had the experience of having their cooking improved by using professionally inspired equipment, whether it is heavy even-heating cookware, good sharp knives, a convection oven, or a powerful-burner range. This has led them to further covet other professional or specialty equipment, some of which is now available at a price.

These "specials" allow cooks a different kind of opportunity to do exactly the kind of cooking they want to do. Some of these unusual cookers are still-expensive constructions, although committed cooks with unlimited budgets may wish to find places for them in their dream kitchen.

WOOD-FIRED OVENS

Large wood-fired pizza ovens allow one to cook breads or pizzas in a smoky atmosphere on a commercial scale

Renato Specialty Products sell an Italian pre-fab kit for making a wood-burning brick pizza oven. It retails for between $4000 and $10,000, depending on size. The kit is designed to be assembled on location. They also retail a gas-fired and wood-burning UL (Underwriters Laboratory—an industry safety group) listed oven that is sold with a completely assembled cooking chamber, although this model will still need to be hooked into a chimney and have cosmetic brick or tile facing added. These retail for between $5500 and $17,000, depending on size.

INDOOR WOOD-FIRED OVEN

On a more domestic scale, Earthstone's French-import wood-fired pizza oven is relatively inexpensive at $1600 for the basic unit, not including masonry work on site. It can be installed indoors or outdoors and allows home cooks to do wood-fired baking or grilling.

COMBINATION OVENS

Restaurant kitchens sometimes use combo ovens, which are superinsulated all-stainless-steel combination steamers and convection ovens. In combi-mode they circulate intensely heated steam with a controlled humidity range from 40 to 100 percent. Fish, vegetables, or meat that has been seared on a stove can be finished in seconds or minutes with steam, staying moist and flavorful while it is cooked virtually fat-free. Because the controls are so precise, the oven can also be used for dehydrating. All of this carries a hefty price tag, about $17,000 for a double-sized stacked model.

BARBECUES AND SMOKERS

Cadillac-quality barbecues and smokers are available to the home cook, in sizes capable of holding between 40 and 160 slabs of back ribs, in units that use electricity for the main fuel and controlled wood smoke for flavor. These come as built-in models for kitchen installation or on wheels for outdoor events. They can range in price from $7000 to $20,000, depending on size and configuration. Domestic manufacturers like Weber produce kettle grills and home smokers for the residential market that have smaller capacities but considerably smaller price tags as well.

COOKSTOVE/HEATERS

Other specialty cooking equipment, like wood-burning cast-iron or soapstone cookstoves, or always-warm multi-hob and multi-oven Agas, have long been the cozy province of energy-conscious kitchens in cold climates. Each offer different cooking methods and varying capacities for heating rooms or houses.

CAST-IRON COOKSTOVES. Cast-iron cookstoves are still being produced—by Stanley/Waterford of Ireland, for example—and now feature emission standards that meet U.S. environmental codes. These elegant black iron and chrome models have an old-fashioned charm. They are equipped with a cooktop and an oven with thermostat, as well as a warming oven above, so it is possible to do all the cold-climate cooking on one of these models alone, without resorting to other equipment or fuels. Retail price for a black model equipped with warming oven is about $1850.

SOAPSTONE WOOD-BURNING RANGES AND OVENS.   Tulikivi, a Finnish company, manufactures traditional heaters and cookstoves in West Virginia out of
American soapstone. Soapstone has the ability to retain heat for long periods without becoming too hot on the surface. Traditional masonry mass heaters like Tulikivi
allow homeowners to create a place in their kitchen for a wood-burning furnace that
can heat a whole house as well as function as a cooker. Some models feature wood-
burning bake ovens, cooktops, or a combination of the two (two chimneys are needed for the latter if used at one time). These vary in price, depending on size, heat
output, and design features, but figure on spending at least $5000, exclusive of the
cost of chimney fabrication.

THE AGA.   Agas are extremely heavy, enameled cast-iron, gas-fueled (in Britain
they are also available fueled by coal), superinsulated, always-on stoves. They must
be vented through a chimney or insulated vent pipe, or, if direct-vented, be located
on an exterior wall. The cooktop has insulated covered hobs that lift up for cooking
and are always set at temperature. Similarly, the ovens (there are two or four oven
configurations) are also always on and are set at particular temperatures, one being
just right for baking and another for slow cooking or plate warming.

In Britain these stoves provide welcome respite from cold and damp and often
are hooked up to a water-holding tank, for the auxiliary benefit of producing hot
water. They are expensive stoves (in the range of $5700 for the two-oven model and
$7950 for the four-oven model), but they last for generations and can be a real asset
for those who live in cold climates and do extensive cooking.

FIREPLACE COOKING.   Building a fireplace and chimney is standard mason's work,
and without much more effort one can be designed with a raised hearth and fitted
with a crane or grill for cooking. In Europe, such farmhouse kitchen fireplaces are
often raised to tabletop level and located in walls opposite the table.

Alice Waters has designed an adjustable Tuscan Grill, marketed by Williams-
Sonoma, to fit into fireplaces for home use. Such antique features can give a new
kitchen warmth and charm and provide home cooks with opportunities for innova-
tive cooking.

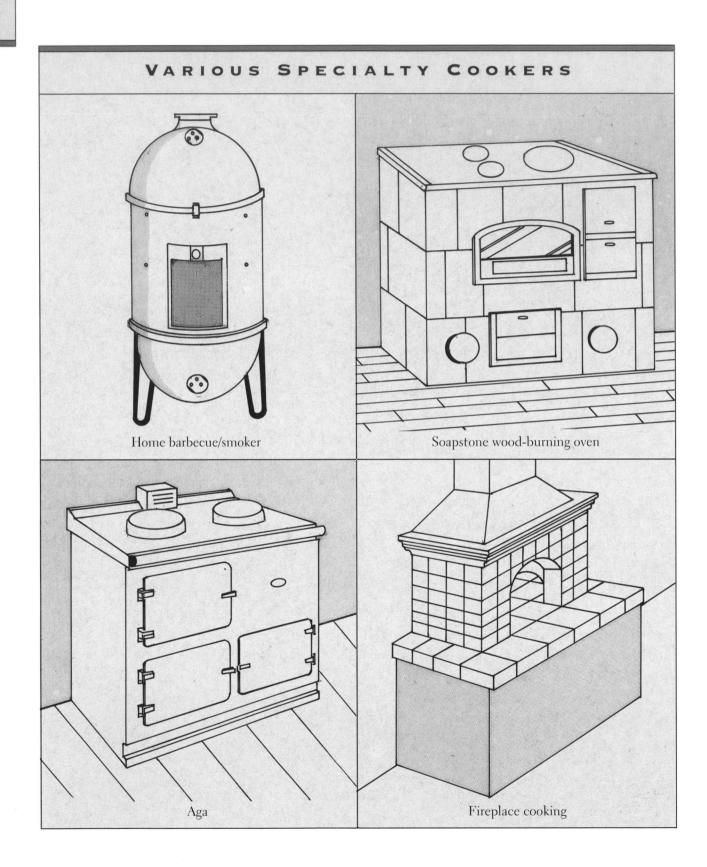

VARIOUS SPECIALTY COOKERS

Home barbecue/smoker

Soapstone wood-burning oven

Aga

Fireplace cooking

HOT MATERIALS

Any countertop material located adjacent to a HOT zone needs to be undamageable by hot pots. Adjacent counters made of ceramic tile (glazed or unglazed), stone (such as marble or slate or granite), or metal (such as stainless steel or copper sheeting applied over plywood) serve the purpose. Other options include solid laminates rated for heat resistance, such as Corian, and wooden, cork, or ceramic heatproof tiles inserted into nonheatproof countertops.

These HOT zone counter areas should be located on both sides of a cooktop or range, as well as be conveniently located for use in resting hot dishes removed from a wall oven and microwave. Remember, too, to provide nearby storage for pot holders.

HOT EXHAUST

Because cooking generates heat, moisture, and odors, all units need exhaust fans that vent to the outside. Commercial kitchens have huge exhaust fans, mounted in hoods that extend above the entire HOT zone, that are on constantly. Such professional equipment serves to remind us that all exhaust systems need to be matched in size and power to the cooking unit.

(Note in this context that "ductless" systems mean that the grease and odor-filled air is not being removed to the outside but only filtered through activated carbon and aluminum, and then returned via a blower. As with filter cigarettes, only some of the potentially hazardous pollutants are removed.)

Domestic cooking equipment manufacturers produce exterior-exhaust units to a roughly common standard, at least in terms of size, so that specialty exhaust system manufacturers, such as Broan, can market vent hoods to fit. As range and cooktop manufacturers create more divergent options, however, such as high-BTU burners on domestic models, it may become more difficult to mix and match venting systems. To capitalize on that concern, many companies that produce cooking equipment also produce venting systems for that equipment, in the form of both overhead hoods and downdraft or raised ventilation systems. In addition to knowing that the parts of a same-manufacturer system are designed to function well together, you will discover other advantages to buying same-brand cooking and venting systems, such as color and style compatibility.

Compatible cooking surfaces and exhaust systems are made not only by domestic manufacturers but also by crossover and commercial dealers. Viking, Five Star, and Russell Range, for example, manufacture overhead exhaust systems that are scaled for the size and BTU output of their cooktop surfaces, and are style- and color-coordinated.

VENTING DESIGN

Vent systems are made in two basic designs, updraft and downdraft, reflecting the direction that cooking fumes are forced to travel.

UPDRAFT EXHAUST SYSTEMS. In an updraft system, the blowers are located within a hood that covers the cooking surface from above. For most effective use, the hood should *cover* the cooking area, not just the rear por- tion of the stove. Fumes and moisture are sucked into the filters via natural convection and by the fan. Note, too, that fans that are remote-mounted on the outside of buildings are considerably quieter than integral interior fans.

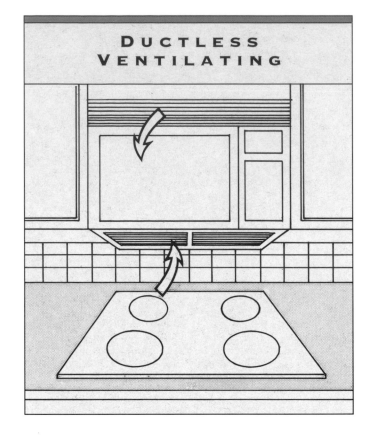

DUCTLESS VENTILATING

Nearly invisible retracting updraft venting systems are available from various manufacturers, including Broan, General Electric, and Gaggenau. Fans are mounted within upper cabinets, and the hood pulls out as needed.

In contrast, extremely visible large overhead units can be turned into design opportunities by using decorative details such as copper or tiles on the hood, or by incorporating pot racks.

DOWNDRAFT EXHAUST SYSTEMS. Downdraft systems can present a visual advan- tage: Because the blowers are mounted below the cooking unit, an overhead hood is unnecessary. (Dacor even has a downdraft island exhaust system that retracts into the countertop surface when not in use.) Smoke, fumes, and odors are sucked via fans into the unit through washable filters and vented to the outdoors. There must, however, be adequate space below the unit and en route to the outdoors for installa- tion. Most experts agree that because downdraft systems have to compensate for the natural tendency of hot air to rise upward, they are necessarily less effective exhaust systems than updraft models.

Exhaust System Safety

With any type of installation it is crucial that grease filters be regularly cleaned (for efficient use and for fire safety), and that venting systems be properly scaled. The Home Ventilating Institute has produced guidelines for determining effective coverage: A wall or ceiling-mounted exhaust fan needs a CFM (moving number of cubic feet per minute) that is twice the square footage of your kitchen. If the cooktop is located on an island with a hood above, the rule is to multiply the length of the cooktop (in linear feet) by 50. If the hood is to be mounted along a wall, the lineal footage of the cooking surface is multiplied by 40. Whatever your dimensions, don't buy any ventilation device with a lower rating than 150 CFM—this is the minimum recommended air-movement number. Be cautious, too, if you live in an airtight or superinsulated home—you will need an air-to-air heat exchanger (which your house should have been equipped with originally if it was well designed) to make using an exhaust fan safe. (Without such a feature, exhausting air could create a vacuum that would suck unsafe emissions from your furnace into the living space of your energy-efficient home.)

Oven Exhaust

It is interesting to note that few producers of wall ovens feature pullout venting systems in their showrooms, product literature, or standard lines. Manufacturers of convection equipment claim that the integral fans in such units perform the same function, even when broiling with a partly opened door.

This is not my experience either when baking or when broiling, and I urge consumers to consider installing a separate venting system above wall ovens. This option, while adding expense to the initial cost of a kitchen, will pay for itself because of the money you will save not having to repaint your walls and cupboards. Such units take up little space; they are unobtrusive, since they pull out from the wall only when in use. Like other exhaust systems, they are either direct-vented on exterior walls or vented via pipe to the outdoors. And again, as with other exhaust systems, the filter needs to be cleaned regularly.

Hot Walls

The walls around a cooking area need an extra measure of protection, both from heat and from grease. An easy-to-wipe-clean surface, such as glazed ceramic tile or stainless steel, is commonly applied to the wall surface. Even stoves with an integral high back, such as commercial and semicommercial stoves, will benefit from additional surface treatment to the portions of back wall and side walls still left exposed anywhere near a cooktop.

Commercial ranges need to be located at least 4 inches from any combustible material—on both sides and to the rear of the unit. It's a good idea for fire safety and air circulation to allow a small airspace around all stoves, including those with zero-clearance ratings. Cautious homeowners who live with high-BTU ovens, whether they are independent wall units or part of a range, might well consider applying additional heatproof foil-backed "chimney flue" insulation along the side of any combustible cabinet adjacent to those units.

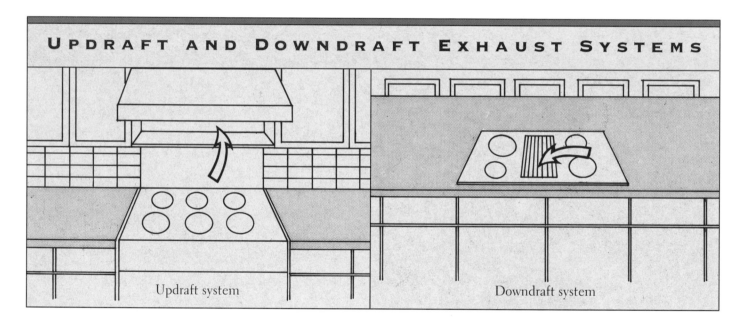

UPDRAFT AND DOWNDRAFT EXHAUST SYSTEMS

Updraft system

Downdraft system

C O L D   Z O N E

MANY FOODSTUFFS ARE UNSTABLE AT ROOM TEMPERATURE AND need to be chilled either to slow down decomposition or to keep them workable. In the latter category, for example, is puff pastry dough, which needs to be kept cool as it is repeatedly rolled and folded. Marble pastry counters are perfectly designed for such COLD preparation activities.

Other kinds of COLD preparation include packaging food for storage in refrigerator and/or freezer and making salads or sandwiches.

Because COLD preparation is so much a part of our daily kitchen activities, it is most usefully located along a counter between the COLD and HOT zones, perhaps between the refrigerator and the cooktop or the refrigerator and the oven (if they are separate), depending on whether the cooks are primarily bakers or cooks. In conventional kitchen layouts, the majority of the counterspace is devoted to COLD/HOT preparation areas. When you are thinking about a new kitchen for multiple cooks (assuming that space is not at a premium), it would be extremely useful to make two such areas and have each devoted to either COLD or DRY, allowing for increased work space around each function. An island that runs parallel or perpendicular to a long counter connecting WET and HOT or COLD and HOT is one such possible functional configuration.

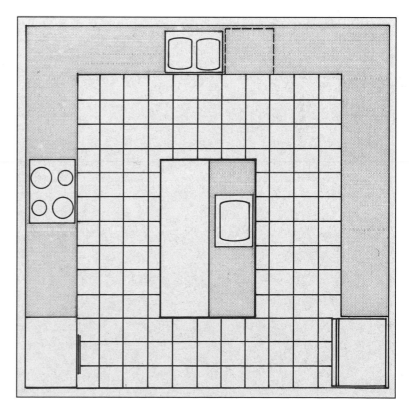

NONELECTRIC COLD ZONE STORAGE

ROOT CROP STORAGE

Historically, a root cellar is a space below ground level for storing root crops (potatoes, carrots, beets, turnips). It is kept cool by the earth's insulating properties. Today, more commonly, a dark corner of a base cabinet that has been fitted with basket drawers to keep it well ventilated is used for the same purpose. Preferably such cabinets should be located on an exterior wall, and not next to a heater.

OTHER FOOD STORAGE

Traditionally, a cool room, passage, alcove, or closet was used as a larder, where cooked foods, cheeses, flowers, fruits, vegetables, and breads were kept cooler than room temperature but not as cold as inside a refrigerated space. Today larders can be built with an electrical cooling unit that maintains a constant 52 degrees, creating a sort of home "walk-in" refrigerator (considerably more energy-expensive than a traditional earth-solar model).

Cool storage closets (perhaps in a foyer) can be used as larders, as can any closed area with a micro-climate that is conducive to keeping its contents cooler than normal house temperature.

Cooks interested in recreating auxiliary COLD storage (and in minimizing their dependence on electrical cooling) have a variety of options: a well-insulated cold box could be constructed on an exterior wall (preferably north or west facing) that has a ventilated door into the kitchen. A more ambitious construction could be an insulated (and ventilated) pantry along a north wall. Basements have long been used for food storage, a solution that works well as long as they are not overheated by a furnace or so poorly insulated that foods are vulnerable to freezing.

Two smaller and less costly solutions, a crawlspace pantry and a cabinet pantry, are described in David Goldbeck's *Smart Kitchen*. Goldbeck also describes traditional California cooling cabinets, which utilize cool air flow from crawl spaces under houses.

COLD EQUIPMENT
(ELECTRIC)

Electric refrigerators and freezers have profoundly affected the ways we shop for food, store food, cook, and eat. Thanks to interstate trucking, supermarket mega-chains, and large refrigerator/freezers, we make a virtue of weekly shopping trips. As a result, much of the food we purchase has been grown thousands of miles away from us, harvested at least a week earlier, and it is destined to age further in our homes before being consumed. These purchasing and diet patterns are actually made possible by the large size of our home-storage facilities, which stand in stark contrast to the amount and variety of cold storage space required when food is seasonally home-grown, harvested as required, or processed for later use as in canning, preserving, pickling, or home freezing.

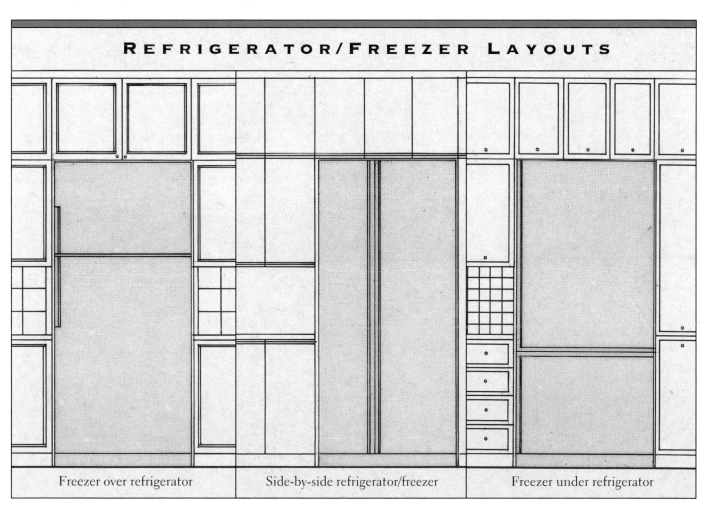

REFRIGERATOR/FREEZER LAYOUTS

Freezer over refrigerator | Side-by-side refrigerator/freezer | Freezer under refrigerator

Cultural expectations play a part in this as well: in most of Europe, where there are still daily marketing traditions as well as regular open-air farmer's markets, refrigerators are generally much smaller than units Americans think of as standard.

REFRIGERATORS

Refrigerators are manufactured in a wide variety of styles and with a range of built-in containers and storage systems. At present, they suffer from a poor energy efficiency record, but this history is about to be challenged, thanks to a consortium of regional power companies who have offered a prize of $30 million, to be awarded in 1994, for an energy-efficient refrigerator design that can be mass-produced and distributed nationally. (The power companies have determined that spending money to encourage production of an energy-efficient refrigerator is cheaper by far than building new power plants.)

Thus far, consumers have shown only limited interest in saving money on efficient refrigeration, but there is hope that with increased awareness and increased choices, consumers may begin to make a difference in the amount of power a household consumes. At present, 20 percent of all of the power used in a household can be traced to refrigerators. And keep in mind that older units are much less power-efficient than newer models. It is for this reason as well that we would be well served to reinvestigate old and energy-wise nonelectric alternatives to COLD storage.

RESIDENTIAL MODELS

Energy-use guides are now mandatory on all new refrigerators, and consumers would be wise to check these carefully before buying. Consumers might also be interested to know that manual-defrost models use 20 to 40 percent less energy than frost-free models. Finally, an astonishing 2 to 4 percent of refrigerator energy loss is due to open-door cruising of the contents by hungry family members! Consider a "menu" posted on the fridge door daily, listing "specials" and suggestions for snacks. ("Today's Snacks: carrot sticks, fruit yogurts, cheese, apple or cranberry juice, left-over pasta salad.")

WHAT SIZE IS APPROPRIATE? The basic (American) rule of thumb for determining the size of the refrigerator you need is to calculate 1 cubic foot per person above a base of 8 to 10 cubic feet (a two-person base line). An additional 2 cubic feet is recommended for those who entertain frequently.

Note that these figures fail to take into account any other cooling space or cool storage areas you may have created, nor do they make allowances for your own particular shopping pattern—some people like to shop daily for COLD items (and therefore need little storage space) and others prefer to shop infrequently (and require larger storage space).

REFRIGERATOR LOCATION.   When locating a refrigerator, keep in mind that it should be placed as far as possible from a heat source, and not in direct sunlight, to minimize the energy required to keep its contents cool.

Some people have devised canny cold-climate ways of using the exhaust heat from their refrigerator: Reasoning that all homes need a supply of fresh air, they locate the refrigerator on an exterior wall and place a small plastic pipe behind and above the refrigerator, which connects the interior wall of the house directly to the outdoors. The pipe opening is fitted with a damper that can be closed should the cold air be too intrusive. When the pipe is open in cool weather, the waste heat from the refrigerator's back coils rises and warms the incoming cold air (which falls) and the house's older and warmer air is pushed by convection currents outside. This heat

REFRIGERATOR PLACEMENT AND MISE EN PLACE

Interestingly, of the three major appliances in a kitchen, the refrigerator is the one for which you have the most flexibility in placement, particularly if you are a cook who assembles all the ingredients before starting a recipe.

This practice, called *mise en place* by cooking professionals, is what divides the pros from the mere players. Assembling and premeasuring (into little bowls) all the ingredients before starting to cook ensures accuracy and aids speed and efficiency. It also allows the refrigerator to be placed somewhat out of the main kitchen traffic path, because it gets opened and emptied less frequently. Instead of being opened over and over again as each ingredient is needed, the refrigerator is opened only twice; once to get out all the ingredients and once to put them back. *Mise en place* makes the whole cooking process go more smoothly, and saves (human and electric) energy.

chimney works as long as the exterior air is cooler than the interior air. When the air inside a house is cooler than the outside (and the occupants want it to remain that way), the damper is closed to prevent infiltration.

INSULATION.   Another criticism of refrigerators as they are presently designed is that they have inadequate insulation, which forces the motor to work harder. To correct this problem, additional rigid foam sheets can be added to the exterior sides, top, and back of a refrigerator with duct tape, leaving the back coils uncovered by fitting the insulation between the coil and the back wall of the refrigerator. Explicit directions for this can be found in David Goldbeck's *Smart Kitchen*.

In any case, remember to leave at least 4 inches of air space behind the refrigerator so that heat from the coils can dissipate, and leave at least 1 to 2 inches of air clearance on each side. Resist the temptation to build shelves directly above the refrigerator—about a foot of air space is needed there as well.

MAINTENANCE.   Refrigerators need regular maintenance to work efficiently. Although few of us actually clean (with a brush or vacuum cleaner) the coils behind and under the unit until we have a problem, they should be attended to twice a year. Drip pans under refrigerators can harbor ever-growing mold collections, which are then blown by the motor exhaust throughout the house; they should be pulled out and cleaned twice a year. Annie Berthold-Bond, author of *Clean and Green*, recommends using a borax solution for this purpose. Interiors of refrigerators can be cleaned with a solution of baking soda and water, and the freezers in manual models should be defrosted regularly.

REFRIGERATOR INTERIORS.   When examining new refrigerators, pay particular attention to the way space is divided inside, considering whether it reflects the way you eat and shop and noticing its degree of flexibility.

Often consumers find built-in containers and shelf storage arrangements less than useful, as they are designed on the basis of pre-set assumptions about how people cook and store leftovers and about what kinds of food they buy. While door shelves sized for cans of soda or beer and areas created for gallon-sized plastic jugs of milk may be extremely useful for those who purchase those items in quantity, these features may be largely irrelevant or even an annoyance to those who shop differently. For such people, a refrigerator with an interior space that can be reconfigured will be a plus.

Glass shelves are both more expensive and more breakable than wire shelves, but they are easy to clean and allow greater visibility throughout the refrigerator.

They do block some air flow, however, because they are solid. Wire shelves aid air circulation and are durable, but they are more difficult to clean.

DEPTH AND DESIGN CONSIDERATIONS. High-end residential manufacturers such as Sub-Zero, KitchenAid, and General Electric produce upscale "built-in" 24-inch-deep refrigerators, 24 inches being the standard base counter depth. Less expensive residential models by these and other manufacturers are produced to the domestic standard of a 30-inch depth. If you wish the look of a built-in refrigerator without paying a premium for a model with a 24-inch depth, you could consider building out adjoining counters and cabinets to the same 30-inch standard. This has the added advantage of providing space for an appliance garage without sacrificing counter area.

Residential refrigerator models are manufactured in a number of styles—options are side-by-side refrigerator/freezer, freezer above the refrigerator (most common), and freezer located in a pull-out drawer below the refrigerator (an arrangement liked more by consumers than manufacturers). Sizes range from 2-cubic-foot below-counter "bar" units to 28-cubic-foot built-in sizes, with fronts that can be customized to match cabinetry.

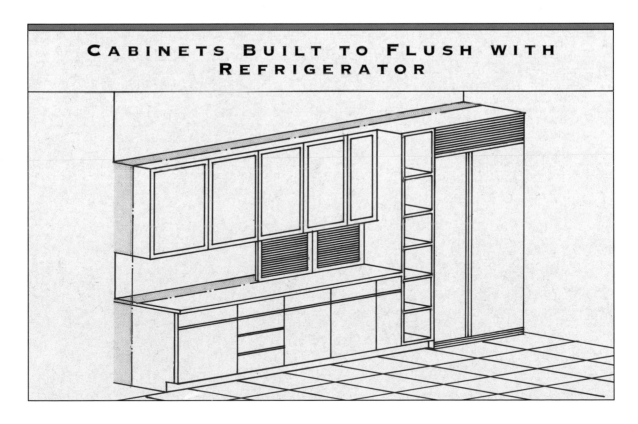

CABINETS BUILT TO FLUSH WITH REFRIGERATOR

Refrigerators also come with a number of convenient (and energy-consuming) options, such as through-the-door ice makers and cold-water spigots, fold-down beverage areas, and continuous ice-making and ice-crushing freezer units. As with all appliances, each consumer needs to decide whether the trade-off for convenience justifies the initial expense of the option and the continuing expense of its operation.

CROSSOVER MODELS

Commercial manufacturers like Traulsen now make crossover lines for the luxury residential market. Like cookstoves modeled on professional equipment, professional and crossover models can offer consumers more options, but at a higher price than a standard residential model (about $5500 for Traulsen's crossover Ultima, and more for the light, commercially rated Ultra). Their Ultima series has been designed with residential use in mind, meets D.O.E. energy use standards (at less than 3.8 kilowats a day, it is equivalent to three light bulbs), and is quieter than strictly commercial and more powerful models. Unlike commercial models, the motor is mounted integrally.

Advantages of such a crossover product include: 24-inch depth by 48-inch width, standard stainless-steel doors (or glass doors for an additional price), stainless-steel door bins, bottom-located pullout crisper compartment drawers, and an automatic ice maker. Traulsen also manufactures a wine cooler with properly tilted wine racks.

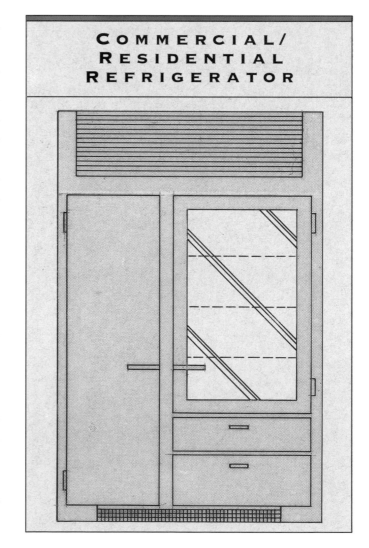

COMMERCIAL/ RESIDENTIAL REFRIGERATOR

COMMERCIAL MODELS

Commercial refrigerators generally are also built to a 24-inch depth, and can have optional glass doors, variable refrigerator/freezer, and wine-cellar spaces built in. They have more powerful compressor motors than domestic models, and are therefore noisier, so it is often recommended that homeowners buying commercial equipment remote-mount the compressor elsewhere—in a basement, for instance—to lower the noise level in the kitchen. If remote mounting is planned as part of the purchase and installation, it need not be much more expensive. Note as well that such a powerful motor also uses more energy. Some commercial models, especially those with glass doors, use more than five times the energy of a residential refrigerator, and therefore cost more to run).

As with restaurant stoves, it is often possible to purchase used commercial refrigerators from resale dealers. When thoroughly cleaned (and rebuilt, if necessary), these powerhouses can provide long service at a considerably lower initial purchase price.

SEPARATE FREEZERS

As with refrigerators, freestanding freezers are less energy-efficient than they could be. Similar considerations in choosing location, leaving air space around them, and adding rigid foam insulation to the exterior all apply (see pages 61–63).

Chest freezers are generally more efficient than uprights, because the contents are less exposed on opening. This advantage is balanced, however, by the relative ease in locating a frozen item in an upright freezer, where all the contents are more visible. All freezers operate more efficiently when full.

PUTTING IT ALL TOGETHER

ORGANIZING SPACE PLANNING BY ZONES MAKES IT EASIER TO ENSURE that there is adequate space for each cooking function. It is also important to look at the relationships between these zones, as well as the relationship of the cook(s) to counter levels and storage height. Floor materials, too, need to be examined in detail. Finally, kitchen design standards merit rethinking in light of all of the above.

SPACE PLANNING

Obviously, you need space for performing WET/DRY/HOT/COLD preparation, as well as space between these areas for appliances. You need space from which to serve the food you have prepared, and space into which you can clear the dishes. You also need cabinet and drawer space for food and/or equipment, and you need to plan for traffic and seating. All these plans will further reflect whether you are one cook cooking alone in a kitchen (in which case you will want a fairly small, efficient plan where you can reach everything with a minimum of effort) or live in a household where friends and family routinely share kitchen work (in which case you will want a kitchen with more clearly defined specialized preparation areas and wide traffic aisles between them). You will also need to make adjustments in space planning if you choose commercial equipment rather than standard residential appliances.

LINEAR COUNTER SPACE

WET: You will need at least 24 inches on one side of the sink (conveniently, this is the width of a dishwasher) for stacking dirty dishes, and at least 18 inches on the other side of the sink for draining dishes. Add these minimum figures to the width of your sink to determine the smallest size of your WET zone.

DRY: For food preparation, a minimum of 3 feet of counter space is necessary for one person. Add an additional 2 feet for each other cook working at the same time. Remember that this is a minimum figure and can easily be expanded if space permits.

HOT: Requires at least 30 to 36 inches on one side of the cooktop or range (for food preparation) and a minimum of 18 inches on the other side (it could easily be the same) to allow for clearance of pan handles, parking of hot pots, and serving.

COLD: A refrigerator requires about 18 inches of counter space next to the opening door (if it is a side-by-side model, allow this clearance on both sides) as a place to set food prior to loading or after unloading the refrigerator.

CABINET SPACE

Standard American base cabinets increase in width in 3-inch increments, starting from 9-inch-wide tray cabinets and going up to 48-inch double-door units. European cabinets are similar in size and incremental scale, although their measurements are, of course, expressed metrically. If standard sizes do not fit your kitchen exactly and you are unwilling to have custom cabinets made for you, it is often possible to purchase "fillers"—or extra pieces of matching stock to mask the gap.

Base cabinets can be fitted with single or double doors hiding retracting or stationary shelves. Another base cabinet option eliminates doors and shelves entirely in favor of drawers of various depths. Many cooks feel that such drawers are preferable to fixed shelves, allowing dishes, pots and pans, and equipment of all kinds to be better organized and more accessible. Retracting shelves, or interior shelves mounted on sliding hardware, are an in-between solution that offers the look of standard doors but the ease of pull-out accessibility. In either case, check to be sure the shelf or drawer is strong enough and well-built enough to support the anticipated weight of your equipment. Nothing is more annoying than drawers with bottoms that warp or collapse under the weight of tools, silverware, or pots. Note that fixed shelves, retractable shelves, and drawers can be mixed and matched to create a kitchen storage system that works best for you.

It is also possible to purchase inexpensive base cabinet "shells" from lumberyards, home centers, and other retailers and then to customize the interiors with separately purchased fittings or hardware. Some of these include Elfa's and Ikea's Swedish-made plastic-wrapped wire drawers, baskets, and shelves, as well as American-made specialized hardware made for raising appliances to counter level, or for holding spice jars or knives in a drawer. You can also transform the appearance of cabinetry in an otherwise well-planned kitchen by stripping the finish off or by painting a new finish on; by resurfacing laminate; or by replacing the cabinet doors.

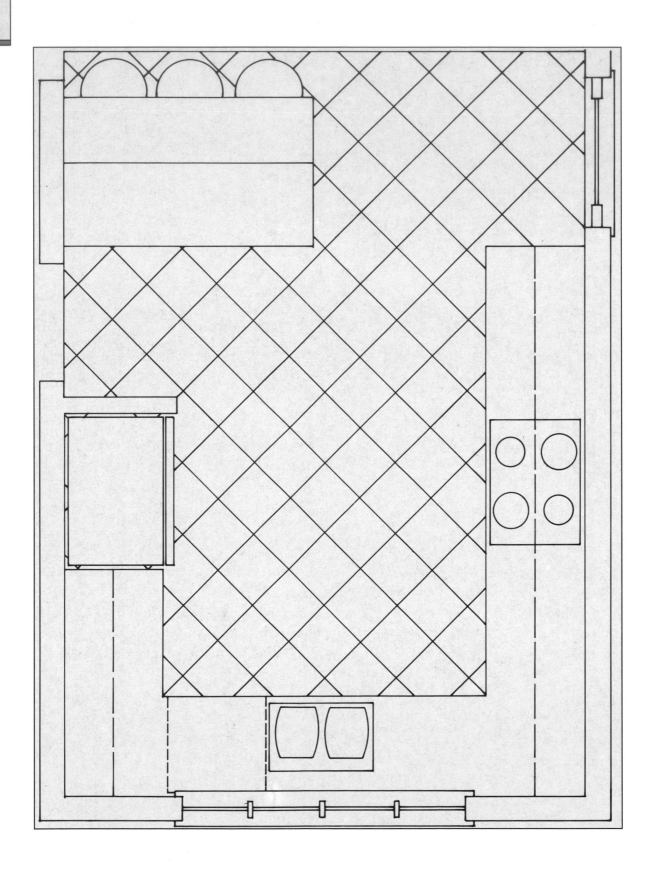

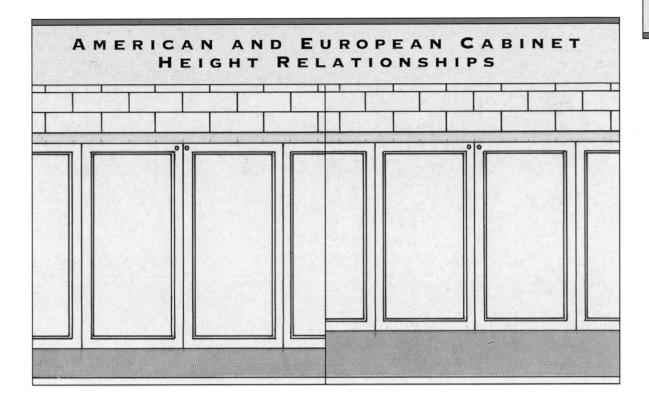

AMERICAN AND EUROPEAN CABINET HEIGHT RELATIONSHIPS

American base cabinets measure 30½ inches high (European standard is 28 inches). Toe plates (or plinths) elevate the counters by 4½ inches (European plinths are higher—usually 7 inches). Typically, countertops add another 1 to 2 inches to the finished height of the counter (standard laminate counters, for instance, add 1⅜ inches). In any case, countertop height usually ends up at the 36-inch-plus mark, unless a designer or homeowner specifies otherwise.

Many Europeans regard their kitchen cabinets and fittings to be personal property that travels with them as they move from house to house or from apartment to apartment. Because these cabinets are meant as portable property, they are designed to be disassembled, and are either plinth mounted (resting on a freestanding base) or wall-mounted. It is then extremely easy to set the base cabinets at an appropriate height for the cooks in the household. Consumers who wish to make their kitchens more responsive to their own needs might prefer to investigate such European sources for stock cabinets, which are less expensive than custom work.

TRAFFIC

For one person in a kitchen, allow at least 38 inches between parallel counters, or between a counter and an island, to provide enough working space. Remember that doors need room to open on both sides. If this aisle functions also as a passage, add 26 inches to allow another person space to walk through (making a grand total of 64 inches between counters).

TABLES AND CHAIRS

Tables and chairs need a minimum passage clearance of 3 feet around them. Thus a 48-inch table needs an additional 36 inches of space around it to allow for (armless) chairs and traffic. Note that this is an extremely minimal measure—when someone is sitting in the chair (add 20 inches), there is not really enough space for another person to squeeze by. A more realistic minimum measure would be 56 inches around a table. (Note that a round table fits into a smaller space better than a rectangular or square table.)

ISLANDS AND PENINSULAS

Islands are freestanding work space, often in the center of a kitchen. A hundred years ago, in pre-industrial "unfitted" kitchens, a central wooden table often functioned as an island (and often was used for dining when not in service for food preparation).

Peninsulas are attached projections running at an angle from existing wall-hugging counters. They offer some of the advantages of an island (increased work space and social contact), but are of more limited use because traffic is directed at the only open end of the peninsula, whereas an island's configuration allows passage on all sides.

CLEARANCES AND DESIGN CONSIDERATIONS

Experts usually maintain that islands need to be at least 2 feet deep and 6 feet long to be functional, although peninsulas can be shorter. My own sense is that an island of almost any size island adds usefulness to a kitchen no matter how small the island is. People who live with tiny kitchens will still be well served by something that can work as an island, such as a small portable work surface on wheels (make sure the wheels have brakes).

Often cooktops are recessed into peninsulas and islands (which can complicate good venting); sinks, too, are frequently seen in such locations, whether they are the only sink or an additional WET area (don't forget to consider backsplash planning in a wall-less location).

Eat-on islands and peninsulas can be variously designed. A portion of the countertop can be lowered to provide a more comfortable location for stools or chairs. Islands can also be built with step-ups (which incorporate a backsplash and a higher, often bar-height counter) to mask the actual activity of the interior, or kitchen, end.

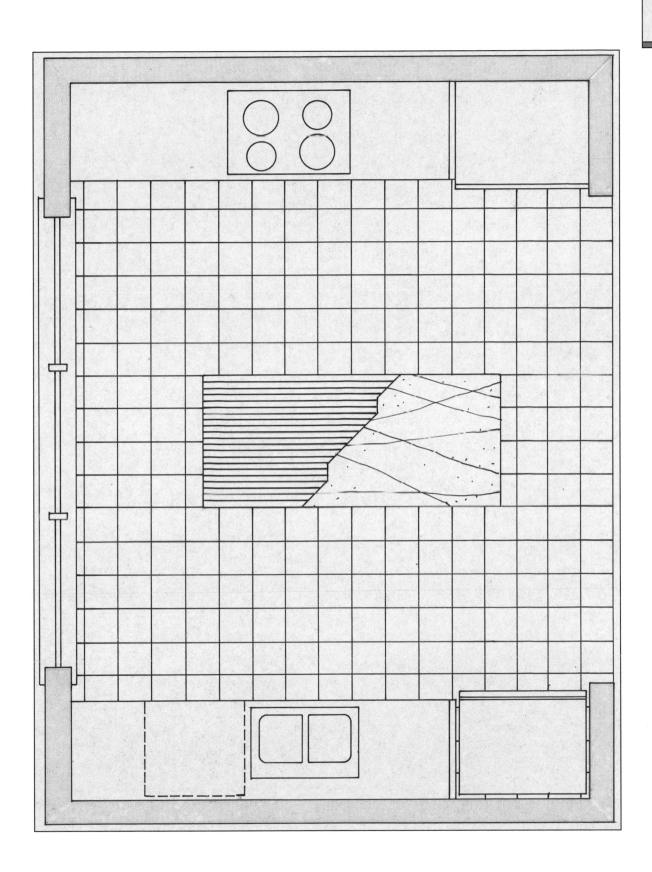

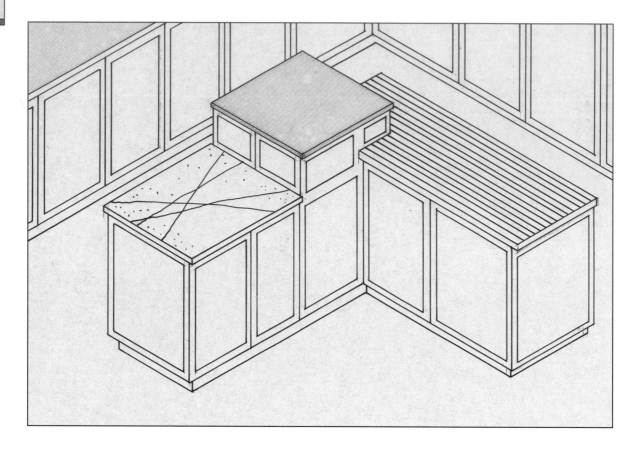

Islands can contain working areas of different heights and counter surfaces, making them a series of custom stations for a wide variety of activities and/or cooks. For example, an island could have part of one long side fitted with a (COLD/DRY) marble slab for rolling out pastry and set at a 30- to 32-inch height. Next to it could be an area of butcher block (DRY), for chopping, at the same low height. The opposite long side could contain a sink (WET) at a standard height of 36 inches, or increased to 38 inches, set into a laminate countertop provided with a backsplash. One of the short ends of this island could be fitted with an overlap or base cabinet cut out to provide leg space for stools in a small eat-in area, or to create a zone for children's participation in the food-preparation process.

FLOOR MATERIALS

It can hardly be emphasized enough that kitchen floors have to be easily cleanable. As with countertop materials and sinks, flooring choices involve such issues as visibility of dirt, frequency and method of cleaning, and hard versus softer surfaces.

CARPET AND RUGS

Carpet is a poor choice of kitchen flooring material because it is difficult to keep clean and will provide a permanent record of grease spills.

Throw rugs, however, particularly those that can be tossed into the washing machine, can provide a note of softness and/or color in front of the sink or cooktop, greatly adding to the charm and comfort of the room.

WOOD

Wood flooring is resilient, is a replenishable resource, and has a surface that can be sanded and renewed. Because wood is highly vulnerable to water (which stains and rots it), it is not a good choice for flooring material near a sink. It could, however, easily be used in a kitchen in combination with a more impermeable flooring material for the WET area, such as a ceramic tile inset, provided that the point at which the materials changed was fairly far from the WET area.

ROLLED FLOORING

Sheets of vinyl and linoleum have long been inexpensive and fairly durable flooring materials for kitchens. Their main advantage is that they are seamless, so that a wooden subfloor is well protected from water damage.

German-made old-fashioned linoleum (composed of linseed oil, cork, wood flour, resin binders, and dry pigments) is currently available in a nontoxic version. It is fairly expensive ($25.50 a square yard) and may be difficult to find (try specialty "eco-stores" selling environmentally responsible products or buy it directly from the manufacturer—see Sources). It is available in a wide range of soft colors.

Standard vinyl (petrochemically based) rolled flooring, often referred to as linoleum but made from very different materials, is available in both waxed and no-wax finishes and in a variety of colors and patterns that either imitate the appearance of other materials (tile, wood, stone) or are frankly manmade.

LINOLEUM AND VINYL TILES

Nonasbestos linoleum is also available in tile form, as are the more widespread vinyl tiles. They are many designs, finishes, weights, and price ranges, with expense frequently being a gauge of durability. Inexpensive tiles often wear less well than heavier tiles of higher quality, which also tend to have their color or pattern more integrated into the body of the tile rather than printed on the surface. Glues used to attach tiles to a subfloor can cause allergic reactions, and ecologically aware consumers may object to the materials used in their manufacture.

RUBBER TILES

Rubber tiles have sound-dampening attributes and are resilient, waterproof, and foot-cushioning. The main disadvantage of rubber flooring is that current manufacturing practices include bumps or grooves along the surface. This makes a rubber floor safer and less slippery when wet, but creates a real difficulty in cleaning. For this reason, they are not recommended for kitchens, where there are often food spills.

CORK TILES

Cork has long been used as a kitchen flooring material in Europe but is less common in America. Cork floor tiles are compressed cork glued with binders and then coated with urethane, which may present out-gassing problems for the chemically sensitive. However, urethane-coated cork deserves a much wider use—it combines well with wood in a kitchen, it looks natural, it absorbs sound and is soft and warm underfoot, dishes don't shatter when dropped on it, and it is well priced.

HARD FLOOR TILES:
CERAMIC, MARBLE, SLATE, BRICK

Hard flooring materials like ceramic, marble, slate, and brick are durable, luxurious, and classic. Although hard tiles are easy to keep clean with a damp mop, the grout between tiles is often a problem. Whether sealed or unsealed, colored or left plain, grout is vulnerable to stains, and because it is lower than the surface of the tile, it often acts as a gutter for dirt.

Stone and clay tiles are so hard that any glass or china that is dropped will shatter. Quarry tiles, too, can crack when heavy pots are dropped on them. Sound is also amplified. Hard tiles are cold underfoot, a disadvantage in cold climates but a plus in warm ones. In many parts of the country, stone or clay tiles are expensive to purchase or install. But, many people, no matter what their climate, value hard tiles for their beauty above these other considerations.

RETHINKING
KITCHEN DESIGN STANDARDS

If we were to walk today into an untouched kitchen of the 1940s, it would be a surprisingly familiar experience, even though the actual materials and aesthetics might be different. Countertops and cabinets would be set at familiar heights, and the placement of lights aimed at the counters and stove would feel familiar too. Remarkably, in spite of the fact that our notions of family, home, and gender-linked activities have undergone profound transformations in the last fifty years, we are still living and working within 1940 standards of basic kitchen design.

Interestingly, theories of good kitchen design were created by such idealistic late-nineteenth-century social reformers as Catharine Beecher (sister of Harriet Beecher Stowe), who came up with the idea that more efficient spaces for meal preparation could enable women to work better. Time-and-motion experts like Lillian Gilbreth (of *Cheaper by the Dozen* fame), who worked in the 1940s, developed the idea of streamlined efficiency further. Much social engineering theory elaborated the appropriate placement and design of kitchens, in hopes that efficient space planning would free women to do the same kitchen tasks in less time.

Partly because of such studies, kitchen cabinets began in the 1930s to be manufactured in sets that were designed to be hygienic, create a unified appearance, and produce a home-laboratory–like work space. By the 1940s, the design and dimensions of appliances and cabinets had become standardized along this "domestic science" model.

The fact that these standards are old would not matter if they still worked, but they fail us often. No longer do we invariably find one average-size woman working alone in the kitchen cooking three-or four-course family meals, and even when we do, we see that one standard counter height often does her a disservice.

STANDARD MEASURES

STANDARD COUNTERTOPS	OVERHEAD CABINETS
HEIGHT: 36 inches	HEIGHT: 30 inches
DEPTH: 24 inches	DEPTH: 9 to 12 inches
	DISTANCE FROM COUNTERTOP: 15 to 20 inches

What follows are some suggestions for rethinking and recreating the "standard" so as to make your own kitchen more appropriate for *you*. (I am indebted to Barbara Kafka for raising my consciousness on this subject, making it impossible for me to continue to ignore my own discomfort in spite of the fact that I am the height that "average" kitchens are designed for.)

To tell whether your countertop and cooking surface are set at a comfortable height, look at your shoulders as you work in your kitchen. Are they up around your ears? When you chop vegetables, is your elbow skewed to the side? When cooking at the range, can you easily see down into a big stockpot? Does your wrist hurt when you shake a sauté pan full of food? Do you often have kitchen accidents? Are there chopping scars on your fingertips, or burn marks down your arm?

HOW TO FIND YOUR CORRECT COUNTER HEIGHT

Experts suggest that your own personal "ideal" countertop height can be determined by measuring the distance between your bent elbow and the floor.(The *average* bent-elbow height for a woman is 35 inches, and for a man it is 39 inches.)

In general, 3 inches below this bent-elbow distance is the best height for most of your countertops. (This would make 32 inches the best counter height for an average woman, and 36 inches the best for an average man. Note that the standard dimension in kitchens of the last fifty years is a 36-inch-high countertop.)

Note, too, that some tasks—such as kneading or rolling out dough—demand even lower countertop areas. These tasks, which are made immeasurably easier by being able to lean into the job using the spine and body weight, are best done on counters that are 3 to 4 inches below a "normal" counter height, or 6 to 7 inches below bent-elbow level (for an *average* woman, this COLD or DRY kneading/rolling area would then be around 28 to 29 inches off the floor). Interestingly, this is exactly dining table height. No wonder that in traditional "prelaboratory model" kitchens the dining table also served admirably as a central worktable!

CHANGING AND CHALLENGING USUAL HEIGHT INSTALLATIONS

With the exception of dishwashers (which at present have only small-tolerance height adjusters for leveling purposes) and one-piece ranges (some of which have the same), all other kitchen equipment can be permanently installed at a comfortable height for the people who work in that kitchen.

Cooktops, for example, can easily be lowered or raised to suit the convenience of the cook. Sinks, too, can be custom-fitted to the kitchen's inhabitants, particularly when the installation of this equipment is part of a kitchen renovation or new construction. The depth of a sink has a profound effect on comfort, and some experts suggest that such WET zone equipment be raised 2 inches to alleviate fatigue when standing, or be fitted with a kneehole for sitting on a stool.

WALL-OVEN PLACEMENT

The placement of wall ovens, too, can profit from rethinking. When they are placed too high in a wall (as in a conventional installation), burns are inevitable for shorter cooks. Consider mounting a wall oven at a height centered slightly above the countertop, taking up a portion of the base cabinet, counter area, and perhaps some of the upper cabinet area as well. This placement allows cooks to see inside most easily, and prevents removing hot food at an awkward angle. Wall ovens mounted entirely below the counter, as in a conventional range position, are at best a space compromise. Bending down and reaching into such an arrangement is awkward and dangerous, and can only be excused when counterspace is at a premium.

MICROWAVE POSITION

The placement of microwave ovens can also profit from consideration—too high a wall-mounted position invites burns and accidents. In this context I must again admit to uneasiness about the microwave's emissions (we notice, for example, that it interferes with the radio when both are on). Our microwave is located in the out-of-the-way pantry, and we make sure everyone is at least 3 feet away when it is on. It rests on a countertop, with space around it on all sides for ventilation.

TEMPORARY MEASURES TO CORRECT INAPPROPRIATE HEIGHT INSTALLATIONS

There are a number of less-than-permanent ways to correct for badly planned work spaces. Countertops that are too high for one or more of the cooks in a kitchen can be accessed by step stools. These can even be made as pull-outs from the toe space or plinths and could be created so as to be at different heights at different work stations.

Another solution from restaurant kitchens is a skid made of slatted wood, which allows cooks to be raised about 3 inches off the floor plane, and further allows spills to sink below the footpath. The skid is picked up for floor cleaning and can even be stored in a closet on its side, if necessary.

Counter areas that are too low for tall cooks can be raised by the addition of another layer of countertop laid on top of the existing one, or by large cutting boards taken out as needed and laid on the counter. Ranges can be raised with blocks to create a HOT surface more comfortable for taller chefs.

OVERHEAD CABINETS

The usual height at which overhead cabinets are placed often leaves the top shelf inaccessible to anyone shorter than average and puts everyone in the kitchen at jeopardy of head injury via open doors. One solution to such collisions is to have open shelves; another is to mount cabinet doors on side-by-side sliders or to make them retract into the sides of the cabinet.

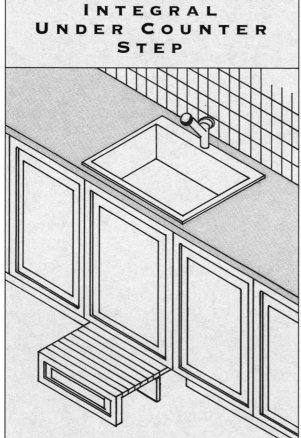

INTEGRAL UNDER COUNTER STEP

OBSTACLES TO CHANGE

There are several major obstacles to creating a kitchen with different height (and differently surfaced) counters, it seems to me. First, we have become accustomed to seeing kitchens with components that are as carefully matched as the shoes and handbags of a typical fifties wife. We have little experience even looking at kitchens with varying materials and counter heights and a strong and functional personal style. We are also unaccustomed to thinking about our own needs and are often at a loss as to how to identify them.

Second, we have practical concerns: Kitchen renovation can be an extremely expensive proposition, and we are uneasy about investing in a kitchen that may end up being too idiosyncratic for resale purposes. What if the next owner of our house has very different measurements and cooking requirements? Don't we need to plan for that hypothetical buyer as well?

I think that a well-planned kitchen that works well for the people who use it has an appeal that transcends mere appearance. Such kitchens invite serious cooks into them and support any changes they may need to make them functional for the next person. As we tour the kitchens that follow in this book, and we see increasingly personal and functional kitchens being created in the future, our sense of what is beautiful, functional, and permissible will inevitably expand.

PART TWO

REAL COOKS, WORKING KITCHENS

...

A PERSONAL APPROACH

AVID HOME COOKS

LISA AND LOU EKUS

LISA AND LOU EKUS ARE COOKBOOK PUBLICISTS AND PRINCIPALS IN their firm, Lisa Ekus Public Relations. As the foremost PR firm in the cookbook field, they are in the enviable position of knowing, hosting, and eating with some of the best cooks and food authors in the country. Their business is run from a building on their property, and their home kitchen often functions as a testing site for recipes in

LEFT: THE CENTRAL WORK STATION ON THE WALL THAT DIVIDES THE EKUSES' KITCHEN FROM THE DINING ROOM FEATURES A BUILT-IN MICROWAVE, A LOWER-THAN USUAL WORKTOP, AND TWO EVEN LOWER PULLOUTS FOR CHILDREN AND OTHER SHORTER COOKS. THE SECOND SINK AND DISHWASHER ARE BUILT INTO THE ALCOVE AT REAR. ABOVE LEFT: TO THE LEFT OF THE STOVE, A DEEP SPICE CABINET FEATURES AN INSERT WITH SHELVES ON BOTH SIDES THAT OPENS OUT LIKE A PAGE IN A BOOK. MORE SPICE SHELVES LINE THE INTERIOR OF THE DOOR AND THE BACK WALL OF THE CABINET. ABOVE RIGHT: THE BOOKSHELVES ARE MOUNTED ON A HINGE, HIDING DEEP STORAGE FOR LITTLE-USED SPECIALTY COOKWARE.

progress, as well as a site for the media training they do for authors about to go out on tour.

When they renovated the nineteenth-century house's much-remodeled kitchen in 1988, they deliberately created a kitchen that could function for everyday family use as well as meet the standards of any chef accustomed to restaurant cooking.

Lou, who is a Renaissance man when it comes to mastering a subject he has previously known little about, took on the job of designer. (He now consults on kitchen design and is amassing a portfolio of kitchens he has created.)

Researching materials and space use led him to conclude that the single work triangle just doesn't make sense. Instead, he created a kitchen that has many triangles and many separate work zones, allowing a number of serious cooks to work in harmony.

There are two WET zones, for example, one at each end of the kitchen. The custom undermounted large single sink and adjacent counter located near the commercial refrigerator are used for food preparation. The other smaller sink is used for table clearing. Each sink has its own dishwasher and garbage disposal, so that food-

ABOVE LEFT: CUSTOM-DESIGNED SHELVES HOLD SERVING PLATTERS ALONG THE END WALL OF THE SECOND-SINK ALCOVE. ABOVE CENTER: THE OVERSIZE UNDERMOUNTED SINK WAS CUSTOM-MADE; THE DRAINBOARD IS ALSO USEFUL FOR WASHING FRUITS AND VEGETABLES. IT IS SURROUNDED BY GRANITE COUNTERTOPS; THE BACKSPLASH IS CERAMIC TILE. ABOVE RIGHT: INSPIRED BY APOTHECARY FURNITURE, THE SECOND-SINK ALCOVE FEATURES MULTIPLE DRAWERS AND ANOTHER PULLOUT FOR AUXILIARY WORK SPACE. BELOW: THE MAIN SINK AREA OF THE KITCHEN WAS EXTENDED IN THE RENOVATION TO ALLOW FOR A BROAD BANK OF WINDOWS CENTERED UNDER A SHED ROOF WITH SKYLIGHTS. A TIN CEILING ADDS TEXTURE TO THE VISUAL MIX. RIGHT: IN THIS VIEW FROM THE DINING ROOM INTO THE ADJACENT KITCHEN, THE GLEAMING RESTAURANT RANGE FITS INTO A WELL-LIT ALCOVE. LIGHTING THE MASSIVE CHERRY DINING TABLE IS A LAMP DESIGNED BY THE OWNERS. TOTEM PIGS COVER THE DRY SINK, BUT ARE ONLY A SMALL PART OF THE EKUSES' PORCINE COLLECTION.

preparation bowls can be washed and stored on one side of the kitchen, while serving pieces, crockery, and glassware are washed and stored on the other side.

The HOT zone comprises a long windowless wall that is capped by an industrial exhaust fan. It houses a massive restaurant stove and also encompasses a restaurant wok, which has 125,000 BTU burners for searing stir-fries. Granite counters at each end of the HOT zone provide heatproof surfaces and shelter chopping board pullouts on each side. These pullouts function in two ways: In addition to providing a surface for cutting, they also provide a lower counter area for shorter cooks. Cabinets above these granite counters provide, on one side, spice cabinets and on the other side additional equipment storage. Under the counters are pots and pans, with baking racks and trays hidden in some clever storage near the preparation sink.

Other ingenious ideas include a narrow series of horizontal shelves used for serving platters; a similar series of cubbyholes for linens in a hallway closet; and a hinged false wall in the kitchen that holds cookbooks on one side. The cavity behind the bookshelves is used for specialty pot-and-pan storage.

Along a short wall opposite the HOT zone is a lower counter with its own even lower pullout. This houses a microwave oven above, with a space for storage and pullup stools below. The area functions as a message center, an eat-in site, and the children's cooking area. Sally and Amelia Ekus find it suits them very well.

The bulk of the Ekuses' enormous cookbook collection is housed in a variety of other spaces: most-often-used volumes are in the kitchen, along built-in shelves near the preparation sink and the back stairs that border the HOT wall. A large floor-to-ceiling set of library shelves divides part of the kitchen from the dining room, and they overflow with often-consulted volumes as well. Cherished inscribed and autographed cookbooks live upstairs in the guest rooms, where insomniac visitors can page through them, imagining what they might cook in the kitchen below.

BELOW: LISA AND SALLY (LEFT) AND LOU AND AMELIA (RIGHT) PEEL LO-CALLY GROWN SPITZENBERG APPLES FOR PIE. RIGHT: OFTEN-CONSULTED COOKBOOKS ARE ARRANGED ON SHELVES THAT TURN THE CORNER FROM KITCHEN TO DINING ROOM, WHERE AN ANTIQUE BARBER'S CHAIR PROVIDES A COMFORTABLE PERCH FOR RESEARCH.

MARYA AND SVEN HUSEBY

MARYA AND SVEN HUSEBY HAVE SPENT MOST OF THEIR PROFESSIONAL lives associated with the Putney School. Sven, a historian, is now the director; Marya, a dancer, is the sales representative for student-made Elm Lea Cheese, sold at Dean & DeLuca in New York, as well as at a southern Vermont location. Marya has always been an avid cook, baking her own bread and cooking with the produce of her garden and orchard. These days her kitchen also accommodates parties to welcome new students and their parents, as well as old friends of the school.

The Husebys started building their Norwegian-style home in the 1970s, felling trees from their own land to make the timbers. Drawing upon Sven's ample carpentry skills, as well as style conventions of his ancestral Norway, they have created a home that magically reflects both the realities of the Vermont countryside and the idealized charm of old Nordic houses.

PREVIOUS PAGE: CANDLELIGHT AND SUNLIGHT ILLUMINATE THE PINE-CLAD INTERIOR OF THE HUSEBYS' KITCHEN–DINING ROOM. THE CHEESE ON THE TABLE AND THE BREADS ON THE COUNTER ARE PRODUCTS OF THE PUTNEY SCHOOL.

LEFT: THE TABLE AND CHAIRS ARE NOR-WEGIAN ANTIQUES, THE CHANDELIER IS A FRENCH REPRODUCTION, AND THE WINDOW LACE IS FROM INDIA, BUT ALTOGETHER THEY CREATE A REMARK-ABLY NORDIC EFFECT. THIS DINING END OF THE KITCHEN IS DOUBLE HEIGHT (BORDERED ABOVE BY A BALCONY-HALLWAY OFF THE BEDROOMS). FLOOR-TO-CEILING WINDOWS ON ONE SIDE OF THE ROOM ARE BALANCED BY THE LARGE OPEN FIREPLACE (AND WOOD STOVE) ON THE OPPOSITE WALL. RIGHT: THE BIG-TICKET ITEM IN THIS KITCHEN, A BLACK AND STAINLESS-STEEL RESTAURANT RANGE, IS CAPPED BY A CUSTOM-MADE COPPER EXHAUST HOOD. NEXT TO IT, A STANDARD MID-LINE DOUBLE SINK SERVES WELL.

One enters the house through the kitchen, which is very much the heart of their home. Two stories high to its rafters, it boasts a professional range, an enameled cast-iron Norwegian-made wood stove for heating purposes (and the odd kettle), and an open hearth for cooking. All the cabinetry is made from a butternut tree that originally stood on the site of the house, and the table and chairs are Norwegian antiques inherited or imported by the family. High above the kitchen, draped over the railing that defines the balcony/hallway, are daughter Kaia's traditional Norwegian linen and cotton handwoven banners.

The kitchen, which is essentially a galley with a parallel island, gains great charm by the addition of large divided-light windows, which illuminate the cooking and dining spaces and provide meadow and forest views. The light will be slightly compromised, but the efficiency of the layout will be greatly improved, by the addition of a narrow marble shelf/counter that Marya is planning to use as additional counter space and as a breakfast bar on the south window side of the stove. This

expanded HOT zone will free the counter space between cookstove and sink to become part of an enlarged WET area. The island, which faces the dining table, is used both for serving and for DRY food preparation.

Unconventionally, the refrigerator is located at the end of the adjoining pantry, which is filled with lace-trimmed shelves holding Marya's china collection as well as foodstuffs. The large mudroom/entry functions as auxiliary COLD storage, housing chest freezer, baskets of produce from the garden, and the firewood their son Johs splits for the stoves.

The house is surrounded by vegetable and flower gardens, a home orchard, and beyond the biggest barn, grazing for the Norwegian fjord ponies they raise as a sideline.

ABOVE: THE FIREPLACE IS FLANKED BY TWO ANTIQUE NORWE-GIAN CHAIRS, EACH MADE FROM A SINGLE LOG. THE JOTUL CAST-IRON WOODSTOVE AT LEFT IS A PRIMARY HEAT SOURCE; THE TOP SURFACE CAN BE USED FOR COOKING. BELOW LEFT: INSIDE THE PANTRY, LACE-EDGED UPPER SHELVES HOLD MARYA'S CHINA COLLECTION AND FOODSTUFFS. THE REFRIG-ERATOR IS OUT OF SIGHT, ON THE END WALL. BELOW CENTER: OLIVE OIL SENT BY FRIENDS IN ITALY SITS NEXT TO VERMONT-GROWN GARLIC. BELOW RIGHT: IN THE WINDOW ALCOVE NEXT TO THE STOVE, A RACK HOLDS CHERISHED COPPER POTS.

ANNICK LEYMARIE

APPROPRIATELY FOR A PLACE DEVOTED TO AN IDEALIZED MEMORY, Annick Leymarie's kitchen reminds us, in contrast to our too-often-seen laboratory model, that kitchens are often the locus of intimate conversation, of security, sentiment, and delight.

Her kitchen also serves notice that the assumptions we often make about what is necessary to furnish a kitchen are in fact arbitrary, culture-bound, and influenced more by equipment manufacturers and media than by our heart's and hand's true desires.

Annick, an avid cook, notable hostess (invitations to her legendary formal dinner parties are coveted), and French teacher, bought this wooden former church in 1980 after it had been used for some time as a barn. Starting from scratch, she installed windows, interior walls, and floors in the vast building, in an attempt to respect the integrity of the well-built structure and to create her ideal home.

The kitchen, which is to her the most important room of the house, was the first space to be completed. Like the rest of the home, it features architectural ele-

PREVIOUS PAGE: ANNICK LEYMARIE'S ENAMELED STOVE IS AN EARLY GAS STOVE THAT FEATURES A WARMING OVEN AND WARMING SHELVES. AT RIGHT IS A WOOD-BURNING COOKSTOVE. A CERAMIC-TILE FLOOR INSERT DEFINES THE HOT ZONE. ABOVE: OPPOSITE THE HOT ZONE IS THE ONLY FOOD-PREPARATION AREA—A LARGE OWNER-DESIGNED MAPLE-TOPPED WORKTABLE. RIGHT: THE WALL-HUNG BASKET NEXT TO THE TABLE HOLDS CLOTH NAPKINS BETWEEN MEALS. THE LITTLE BROOM IS USED FOR CLEANING OFF THE WORKTOP. FAR RIGHT: ABOVE THE WOODSTOVE, A SET OF COPPER SAUCEPANS THAT ANNICK INHERITED FROM HER GRAND-MOTHER HANGS FROM A PINE SHELF.

ments salvaged from other homes in the area, as well as furnishings, tools, and equipment selected in response to a fine-tuned antique-loving design sense that will accept only what is right for the room. As a result, she has created a kitchen that is in every sense unique and yet alludes to a whole variety of traditional French kitchens.

The kitchen was designed with particular materials and preparation zones in mind. The

FAR RIGHT: THE PAINTED UPPER CABI-
NET WAS A FLEA-MARKET FIND, AS WAS
THE DRAWER IN THE LOWER UNIT,
WHICH WAS CUSTOM-BUILT TO FIT.
RIGHT: ANNICK'S OWN BREADS AND AN
APPLE TART REST ON TOP OF THE WOOD-
STOVE. BELOW RIGHT: PARKED ABOVE
THE THRIVING VEGETABLE GARDEN, A
GAILY PAINTED HOMEMADE GYPSY
WAGON IS USED AS GUEST QUARTERS.
BELOW: A WELL-PLANNED WALK-IN
PANTRY WAS BUILT IN ONE CORNER OF
THE KITCHEN. IT STORES CHINA, FOOD,
AND WINE. OPPOSITE PAGE: ENCLOSED
IN A TILED ALCOVE, AN ANTIQUE DOUBLE
SOAPSTONE SINK ANCHORS THE WET
ZONE. HIDDEN IN THE ALCOVE WING AT
LEFT IS THE DISHWASHER; AT RIGHT IS A
SMALL REFRIGERATOR.

WET zone, in the form of an antique stone sink, is confined to a specially built alcove framed by an archway, and it is tiled in the French manner, with white tiles intersected with cobalt diamonds. The wings of the alcove hide a small European-scale refrigerator on one side and a dishwasher (the top is used for WET preparation) on the other. On the walls above the dishwasher are open storage shelves for everyday dishes and glassware. The right-hand side of the stone sink is covered with a wooden board that contains a removable wooden cover positioned over the compost-collecting bucket. The cotton lace curtain (French looking, but actually the result of a lucky find at an American discount store) under the sink hides washing supplies.

Within the main area of the kitchen there are no conventional cabinets or countertops. Instead, COLD zone storage for food, wine, and china is provided by a closed-off walk-in pantry built into a corner of the space. Food preparation takes place in different locations: the primary DRY zone preparation area is the large custom worktable, which incorporates massive antique wooden legs, a new apron, and a top made of an old maple bowling alley floor. But much kitchen work is also done sitting down in front of the window around the small dining table, which provides a space that is as much social as culinary. In fact, Annick asserts that "kitchen cabinets are a manufacturer's plot to separate women from each other." And it is certainly true that this kitchen encourages a different kind of conversation from what one might have in a space of lesser intimacy.

Neither is there a conventional stove. HOT zone preparation and cooking are done on two different stoves located side by side on a tiled hearth, depending on the season. In summer, late spring, and early fall, the antique gray-enamel gas stove provides cooktop and oven (complete with warming oven above). In colder months, the big black iron wood-burning stove heats room, cook, guests, and food alike. And above the woodstove, hanging from the rafters, there is often a basket that holds the curing chèvre that Annick makes for home use.

Through the French doors off the kitchen (which is one story above the ground) is an ample porch used for warm-weather alfresco dining. From it one can admire the fruit, flower, and vegetable gardens from which produce is taken to enrich the cuisine, and one can watch the three white turkeys that are being raised for their Thanksgiving moment of glory.

CHARLES MORRIS MOUNT

CHARLES MORRIS MOUNT, A NEW YORK CITY INTERIOR DESIGNER, IS A partner in Silver & Ziskind/Mount. Over the years, he has made designing kitchens a particular specialty. His own Manhattan home kitchen, which was designed in 1980, looks as current and functional today as it did when it was first executed.

Charles thinks of kitchens in terms of "the exploded triangle," by which he means the creation of a series of auxiliary work triangles that relate tangentially to a primary triangle. In this kitchen designed for multiple cooks, Charles traces multiple work stations that refer back to the cooktop, ovens, refrigerator, or sink.

LEFT: THE VAULTED CEILING DEFINES CHARLES MORRIS MOUNT'S MAIN GALLEY KITCHEN, BUT A PANTRY, REFRIGERATOR, AND BAKING CENTER ARE LOCATED IN AN ADJACENT AREA. ABOVE RIGHT: THE PANTRY IS AN INTRICATE ARRANGEMENT OF SHELF-LINED DOORS THAT ARE HINGED TO FIT WITHIN A DEEP CLOSET. ABOVE LEFT: PULLOUT DRAWERS SLIDE OUT OF THE BASE CABINETS. THE TWO SALT-GLAZED STORAGE JARS ON THE COUNTER ARE BY MASTER POTTER KAREN KARNES.

The entire black-marble-topped peninsula is used as a primary HOT zone, housing modular cooktop units set one deep along one side. Above this ("placed, unfortunately, too high," reports Charles) is a commercial salamander/broiler. The surrounding cabinets hold all the necessary pots and pans for this zone.

Opposite the HOT zone, a generous sink marks the WET zone, with china and glassware storage above. Counters on each side of this zone function as additional work stations for food preparation, and the aisle between that side of the room and the peninsula is wide enough so that two cooks can pass by easily.

Toward the street, counters beginning under the windows in the kitchen extend into the dining and living areas, making a long series of preparation, serving, and display areas that reach along the length of the room. At the kitchen end, this area functions as a COLD preparation zone and pastry area, from which dough is brought into the wall ovens at the opposite end of the kitchen. The wall ovens face into the kitchen from an auxiliary area that combines pantry, baking station, and cookware storage.

This kitchen has a number of useful ideas, particularly in relation to the HOT zone: the placement of the cooktop burners in a single row allows greater safety for the cook, since there is no reaching across hot burners to gain access to pots in the rear, and the wall ovens are placed at an intermediate height so that the contents are visible and easy to remove.

A generous round marble-topped dining table is located just beyond the peninsula, creating another place for auxiliary cooks to work or companions to linger while work is in progress.

FAR LEFT: GARAGED IN ONE CORNER OF THE KITCHEN, THE TRASH CAN HAS WHEELS, MAKING IT EASY TO CLEAN UP ANYWHERE. LEFT: A CULINARY COLLECTION OF MORTAR AND PESTLES SITS OUT ON THE COUNTER, READY TO BE USED. ABOVE: BECAUSE THE KITCHEN IS OPEN TO THE DINING ROOM, COOKS CAN ALWAYS BE PART OF PARTY. THE LONG LINE OF MARBLE-TOPPED CABINETS THAT CONTINUES INTO THE DINING AREA AND LIVING ROOM FUNCTIONS BOTH FOR BUFFETS AND FOR DISPLAY.

LU AND MAYNARD LYNDON

LU AND MAYNARD LYNDON ARE THE OWNERS OF PLACEWARES (SIX stores in Boston devoted to home organizing and storage) and partners in LyndonDesign, an architectural and design firm. The Lyndons met while working at Design Research in the sixties, and their renovated carriage-house home reflects their long association with, and appreciation of, classic modern Scandinavian style.

Their kitchen functions as a testing area for storage and design ideas: the Finnish drying cupboard has a hidden drainpipe that connects to the sink, making it easy to handwash and put away wet dishes (the Lyndons prefer not to have a dish-

washer). This WET zone occupies the entire window wall. As one turns the corner, open racks and shelves hold serving dishes and casseroles, while other pots and pans are stored in pull-out wire basket drawers in the cabinets below.

Because this kitchen is so well planned, each bend or turn of the counter creates work stations. Counter-top materials change where appropriate (laminate in the WET zone, wood in the DRY zone), and counter heights shift to make it easy for a cook to find the most suitable work area.

The wide central peninsula organizes the kitchen into several different

LEFT: THE CURVED TABLE IS ACTUALLY ONE END OF THE PENINSULA THAT CONTAINS THE HOT ZONE IN THE LYNDONS' KITCHEN. THE SINK IS FLANKED BY A WALL-HUNG DISH DRAIN. ABOVE: AROUND THE CORNER FROM THE PENINSULA, A BUILT-IN KITCHEN DESK STORES WINE. ABOVE IT IS A PASS-THROUGH INTO THE NEXT ROOM. RIGHT: THE REFRIGERATOR IS BUILT INTO AN ALCOVE THAT FORMS THE END WALL OF THE WINDOW SEAT.

zones: The stovetop portion and its surrounding counter are used for HOT preparation. On the other side of that peninsula is a long expanse of counter for DRY zone or COLD zone work, easily accessible to the refrigerator. Perpendicular to this station is another higher area used as a desk or for stool-seated preparation work, while on the far side of the refrigerator a low alcove window seat provides a place to peruse a cookbook, or perhaps to tackle shelling a bowl of green peas.

Kitchens like this one make it both possible and pleasurable for five or six friends or family members to create meals together. They further remind us that working kitchens do more than merely look pretty—they have a complexity that good use inspires.

LEFT: THIS DISH DRAIN HAS A GUTTER PIPE THAT COLLECTS WATER AND DRAINS IT INTO THE ADJACENT SINK. A TAMBOUR DOOR AT THE TOP PULLS DOWN TO HIDE THE DISHES AND SILVERWARE. BELOW: SCANDINAVIAN IN ORIGIN, THE ANTIQUE STORAGE CUBE IS MADE FROM WOOD WITH GLASS DRAWERS. IT HOLDS KITCHEN MISCELLANY AND FUNCTIONS AS A DISPLAY PEDESTAL. RIGHT: ON THE BIRCH STORAGE WALL ABOVE ANOTHER PREPARATION-SERVING AREA, ADDITIONAL WOODEN DISH DRAINS AND OPEN SHELVES HOLD MOST OF THE FAMILY'S CHINA AND GLASSWARE. BOTH THE FLOOR AND THE CABINET PULLS ARE MADE OF RUBBER.

LESLIE ARMSTRONG

THIS NEW YORK APARTMENT KITCHEN WAS DESIGNED BY ARCHITECT Leslie Armstrong to satisfy her two clients' unusual requests: He likes to cook alone, without anyone near him. She also likes to cook. They wanted one kitchen that would work for them both, even simultaneously.

By tearing out an unused maid's room and adding that space to the original kitchen, Leslie created an unusual W-shaped configuration of cabinets and counters. This enabled her to make a galley-style mini-kitchen in one corridor, culminating in a small powder/laundry room, and a storage alley with walk-in closet along the other corridor. This second corridor has the refrigerator built in along its front wall and the

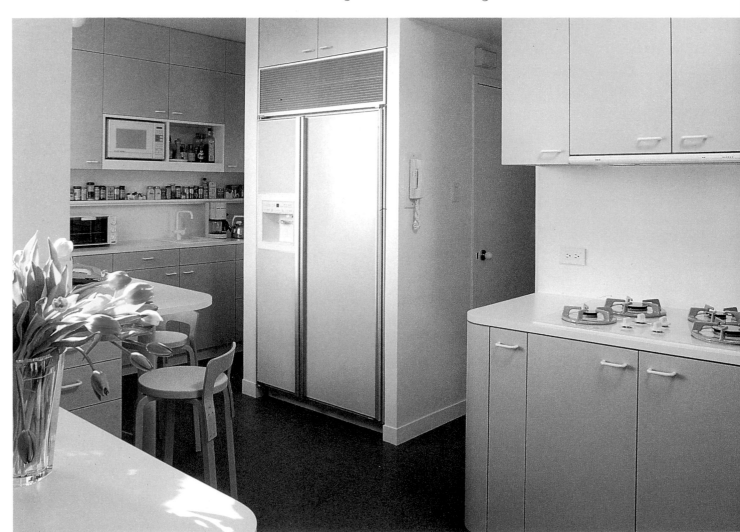

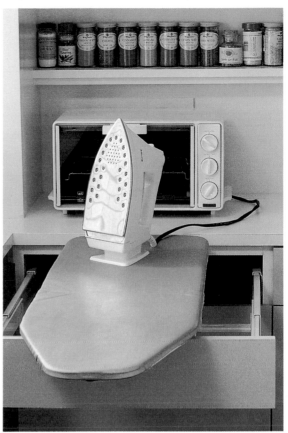

LEFT: AS SEEN FROM THE ENTRANCE, THE MAIN COOKING AREA IN THIS KITCHEN DESIGNED BY LESLIE ARMSTRONG IS IN THE FOREGROUND, AND THE AUXILIARY KITCHEN, WITH A MICROWAVE AND A SMALL SINK, IS IN THE BACKGROUND. THE REFRIGERATOR MARKS THE BOUNDARY BETWEEN THE TWO AREAS, AND THE WINDOW-HUGGING DINING–FOOD PREP COUNTER (TURNING THE COUNTER AT LEFT) TIES BOTH SPACES TOGETHER. ABOVE: PURITY OF FORM IS THE HALLMARK OF LESLIE'S DESIGN, AND HER CUSTOM SHELVES FLOAT AWAY FROM THE WALL WITHOUT VISIBLE SUPPORT. ABOVE RIGHT: CAREFUL SPACE PLANNING ABOUNDS, AND IS EXEMPLIFIED IN THE IRONING BOARD THAT POPS OUT OF A DRAWER. THE AREA IS ILLUMINATED BY NATURAL LIGHT FROM THE ADJACENT (AND NEWLY ENLARGED) WINDOW. RIGHT: THE NARROW CAN-DEPTH CUPBOARD WAS CARVED OUT OF THE CURVED END WALL OF THE COOKTOP CABINET.

service entrance at its rear. The square space of the original kitchen holds a more conventional arrangement of counters, cooktop, ovens, and sink along three walls, while new perpendicular twin windows illuminate the corner-turning eating/work counter opposite that links both areas.

The resulting kitchen not only satisfies all the requirements imposed by the clients, it is also a model of well-planned work zones. Two sinks provide widely separated WET areas, although one is primary and the other is mostly used for making coffee or tea. The husband cooks at the cooktop, undisturbed by the wife, who works

BELOW LEFT: THIS VIEW OF THE HOT ZONE FROM THE MID-POINT OF THE KITCHEN, NEXT TO THE REFRIGERATOR, ILLUSTRATES PREPARATION-ZONE PLANNING AT ITS BEST. NOTE THE SINK AT RIGHT. RIGHT: THE AUXILIARY KITCHEN HAS EVERYTHING THE MAIN KITCHEN HAS, BUT IN MINIATURE—ITS ONLY OVENS ARE A MICROWAVE AND A TOASTER, AND THE COOKTOP IS AN ELECTRIC KETTLE. EVEN THE SINK IS DIMINUTIVE.

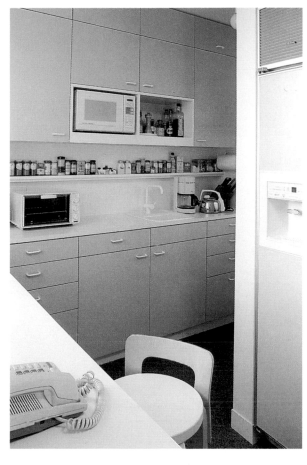

in the area on the other side of the refrigerator. Each has an oven—she uses the microwave, and he the wall ovens. The window counter functions both as eat-in area and as preparation zone, providing a place to work either standing up or sitting down. Ample closed cupboards provide storage for utensils, dishes, silver, and food, while a large closet functions as pantry and utility space. Often-used items sit on open shelves specially designed to hold them.

Because the couple collect art and have high aesthetic standards, colors and surfaces were carefully planned. Matte gray laminate coats all vertical surfaces of the cabinetry, providing a subtle gloss. Counters are white laminate, and the floor is cork tile (which is sound-insulating as well as extremely comfortable underfoot). Open shelves are invisibly mounted and colored the same shade of white as the walls. Their very unobtrusiveness creates a context in which even ordinary kitchen objects stand out like sculpture.

COOKBOOK AUTHORS AT HOME

BARBARA KAFKA

BARBARA KAFKA, COOKBOOK AUTHOR, FOOD ESSAYIST, AND MICRO-wave columnist, believes that every cook has to know himself or herself well before planning a kitchen. She has been cooking in this kitchen of her country house for more than twenty years, and she has made it work perfectly for her own impressive culinary and entertaining styles.

A person of small physical stature, she has lowered her cooktop by 6 inches to make it possible for her to "cook with the big boys," she says, as she shakes a massive sauté pan effortlessly over the low burner. "And I can see into stockpots without standing on my toes," she adds, demonstrating eye contact with the bottom of what surely must be one of the tallest pots to be found in any domestic kitchen.

The kitchen also reflects her concerns for safety: the wall oven is placed at countertop height, as are the three microwave ovens. "Why *three* microwaves?" I ask. "One for jams and jellies, one for the vegetable course, and one for fish," Barbara answers as if explaining the obvious.

Rolling up her sleeves, Kafka displays chef's scars of burns up both her forearms: "From hot fat rolling out of a pan in a too-high oven," she says matter-of-factly. Cuts

LEFT: BARBARA KAFKA'S UNUSUAL PAINTED-FRAME MIR-ROR CAME FROM A HOUSE IN NEWFANE, VERMONT, AND THE ANTIQUE CUPBOARD AT RIGHT IS ALSO A VERMONT PIECE. THIS PART OF THE KITCHEN FORMS AN ELL AWAY FROM THE MAIN LINE WORK STATIONS. RIGHT: THE WOOD-BURNING COOKSTOVE IS LOCATED OPPOSITE THE LONG DINING TABLE, WHERE IT IS USED AS A BUFFET IN WARM WEATHER. TO ITS LEFT IS A HOT-WATER HEATER CLAD IN COPPER. A LARGE BUTCHER BLOCK IS AT RIGHT.

ABOVE LEFT: BITS OF IRONWORK FOUND IN THE BARN HAVE BEEN MADE INTO A POT RACK. ABOVE CENTER: LOCATED JUST OFF THE KITCHEN, THE PANTRY REMAINS JUST AS IT WAS WHEN KAFKA BOUGHT THE HOUSE. SHE USES IT IN THE TRADITIONAL WAY, STORING CHINA, FOODSTUFFS, AND LARGE SERVING AND COOKING PIECES THERE. ABOVE RIGHT: KNIVES ARE CAREFULLY AND SAFELY STORED ON WALL-HUNG MAGNETIC RACKS. THE HERBS AND LETTUCE ARE FROM KAFKA'S GARDEN. BELOW: THE CLASSICALLY ARRANGED RAISED-BED VEGETABLE GARDEN IS CENTERED BY AN URN. RIGHT: THE ORIGINAL EIGHTEENTH-CENTURY KITCHEN IS NOW THE LIVING ROOM, WHERE THE FIREPLACE AND BAKE OVEN (AT RIGHT) ARE STILL USED FOR COOKING.

from knives have also left their scars, and Kafka is now careful to do her chopping at an appropriately positioned counter, as well as to store all knives and scissors on wall racks rather than in drawers.

The kitchen is essentially arranged in a long line, starting with the refrigerator (there is an auxiliary refrigerator and separate upright freezer in the basement below, along with a wine cellar); then comes the counter that runs to the sink; more counter follows; a step down to the cooktop level is framed by a large window that casts generous light on work in progress; and a larger step leads up to a conventional wall oven installed at an unconventional height.

Opposite the HOT zone is the pantry filled with Kafka's china collection, a worktable, and a freestanding old butcher block (under which is the mobile compost-collecting bucket). Around a corner, the massive wood-burning cookstove serves as a buffet in summer and auxiliary heat and HOT preparation zone in winter.

A long table makes the kitchen an eat-in site all year round. The table is framed by an unmatched pair of antique china cupboards and a huge handpainted mirror that reflects the food and company back into the room.

This is a kitchen designed for use by the person who cooks in it; it's not about show or style. The plywood cabinets were in the house when it was purchased, and they haven't been changed. Instead, all the changes in this kitchen over the years have been made either to increase the functionality of the space or to satisfy the collector's delight.

The eighteenth-century farmhouse's original kitchen is now the living room, but the original hearth is still very much in use, and Barbara and her husband light fires in the bake oven to make breads in winter.

LEFT: BARBARA KAFKA AT WORK. NOTICE THE RELATIONSHIP OF THE COOKTOP TO HER HEIGHT, AND HOW EASILY SHE CAN SEE DOWN INTO A TALL POT. THE DOWN-DRAFTING EXHAUST SYSTEM DOES NOT OBSCURE LIGHT FROM THE LARGE WINDOW THAT ILLUMINATES THE COOKING SURFACE. BELOW LEFT: THE TABLE, SET FOR LUNCH, SHOWS OFF SOME OF KAFKA'S CHINA COLLECTION. BELOW: THIS LONG VIEW OF THE KITCHEN SHOWS HOW THE COUNTER HEIGHT CHANGES TO ACCOMMODATE SERIOUS WORK BY A SHORTER COOK.

GIULIANO BUGIALLI

IN A DOWNTOWN MANHATTAN TOWNHOUSE, GIULIANO BUGIALLI has three distinctly different kitchens, each used for very different kinds of work and each embellished with antique and modern Italian elements for display and use.

The largest of the kitchens is on the entrance floor and is visible from the front door when one looks through the gracious dining room toward the rear of the building. This kitchen, with three four-burner restaurant ranges and polished granite counters arranged between them, is the main teaching kitchen. Made splendidly functional by the freestanding and mobile work island Bugialli had made in Florence, this kitchen easily accommodates the cooking master and his students. Sinks and a dishwasher, as well as auxiliary burners, are accessible from the aisle that lines the back wall, hidden away below the rear high counter.

Downstairs at basement level, through a wide corridor lined with heirloom china and cooking equipment, is a whole other teaching (and sometimes domestic-use) kitchen devoted to wood-fired cooking. Encased in two massive brick chimneys at either end of the room are a grill/rotisserie and a traditional brick oven. Here

PREVIOUS PAGE: GIULIANO BUGIALLI'S
MAIN TEACHING KITCHEN FEATURES AN
ALTERNATING ARRANGEMENT OF FOUR-
BURNER RESTAURANT STOVES AND A
GRANITE PREPARATION AREA. ABOVE
LEFT: THE BASEMENT TEACHING KITCHEN
IS USED FOR WOOD-FIRED COOKERY.
ABOVE: IN THE PRIVATE KITCHEN AT THE
TOP OF THE HOUSE, A TOWER OF SMALL
DRAWERS HOLDS DOMESTIC TOOLS. BE-
LOW: AN ISLAND IN THE BASEMENT
KITCHEN HOLDS BOARDS FOR DRYING
PASTA.

Bugialli teaches Italian hearth cookery by student participation rather than by demonstration.

Finally, up two flights of steep stairs, is the smallest kitchen of all: the domestic retreat. It overlooks a two-level fragrant and colorful rooftop garden filled with birds and butterflies (they find it even in Manhattan) and planted with pots of herbs and edible flowers for the table.

Family meals are prepared in this kitchen, and it works well for one or two cooks to use together. It is arranged in a U shape—one side is the HOT zone, one side is the WET zone, and the last side, which is a kind of peninsula, is used for DRY zone and COLD zone meal preparations and is accessible from both sides. The undercounter refrigerator helps to maintain the unbroken line of the granite countertops, and the row of paired antique Florentine wooden doors in the living room hide deep cupboards filled with shelves of food supplies and china.

ABOVE: THE DOMESTIC KITCHEN IS U-SHAPED, WITH DOORS TO THE GARDEN AT ONE END. NOTE THE SINK FACING INTO THE GARDEN. BELOW LEFT: ALTHOUGH THE EXHAUST HOOD IS EVEN LARGER THAN THE STOVE, IT IS UNOBTRUSIVE. THE ANTIQUE FLORENTINE DOORS ALONG THE WALL BEYOND THE KITCHEN HIDE STORAGE AREAS. BELOW RIGHT: INSIDE THE DOORS ARE CHINA, GLASSWARE, AND LINENS, CONVENIENT TO THE SMALL TABLE SET IN FRONT OF THE WINDOWS.

Because the domestic kitchen is built within a much bigger room, and because the U shape is wide and the work zones are so clear, two cooks can easily work together—with others working along the outside counters, if necessary. It is fitting that this is the culminating kitchen of the house, since it uses so well the lessons of the teaching kitchens below.

ABOVE: A WOOD-FIRED OVEN IN THE BASEMENT KITCHEN IS CAPPED BY THE COPPER POTS USED WITHIN IT. LEFT: THE LONG GRANITE COUNTER IN THE BASEMENT KITCHEN IS SURROUNDED BY WORKING STUDENTS WHEN CLASSES ARE IN SESSION.

ARTHUR SCHWARTZ

COOKBOOK AUTHOR, RESTAURANT REVIEWER, AND RADIO FOOD-show host, Arthur Schwartz has cooked his way through many a small and substandard city kitchen. When he finally got a chance to do a kitchen from scratch, he made it reflect all his dreams of an ideal work space.

When he first purchased his country house in Connecticut, it was a modest structure with an all-too-familiar tiny kitchen. With this new kitchen/dining addition designed by architect Robert M. Tieger, the house has more than doubled in size.

The kitchen is designed to be the center of living and of entertaining. Open to the dining room and the living room beyond, it is surrounded by natural light from wraparound above-counter windows, a skylight in the adjacent entrance hall, and light cast down from the new master suite above. All the red birch cabinetry is of

furniture quality (it was constructed by Schwartz's cousin, Granville, New York, cabinetmaker Mark Teller), and the granite that forms the kitchen counter is repeated along selected areas in the dining and living rooms, tying all the spaces together.

The kitchen also sports a couch, a hidden television/VCR, and a cabinet filled with old movies on tape, so that Schwartz's movie-buff companion can be with him in the kitchen as he works. Although the kitchen is designed with one cook in mind, it is easily used by many more, thanks to the careful planning of each work zone.

The kitchen is U-shaped, with a central island. Along one wall there is a baking center, with a large electric oven and baking-dish storage built-in below. Around a corner, a custom-made undermounted stainless-steel double sink defines the WET zone area, with adequate counter space on each side for that purpose. The professional/crossover gas range provides the HOT zone with a center; the oven is used pri-

PAGE 117: THE COUCH IN ARTHUR SCHWARTZ'S CONNECTICUT KITCHEN FACES THE ISLAND FOR CONVIVIAL COOKING. A TELEVISION IS HIDDEN IN THE ISLAND, AND THE CABINET TO ONE SIDE OF THE COUCH HOLDS VIDEOTAPES. PREVIOUS PAGES: BREAKING THE BOUNDARIES BETWEEN A COOKING SPACE AND A SOCIAL SPACE, THE DINING ROOM FLOWS SEAMLESSLY OUT OF THE KITCHEN, SHARING THE SAME SLATE FLOOR, ARCHITECTURAL DETAILING, CABINETRY, AND AMPLE NATURAL LIGHT. RIGHT: THE ISLAND ANCHORS THE KITCHEN, PROVIDING WORK SPACE FROM ALL SIDES. UNDERNEATH IT, OPPOSITE THE STOVE AND SINK, ARE OPEN SHELVES FOR EASY ACCESS TO POTS AND PANS.

marily for roasting. As one turns the last corner, there is a stretch of counter that ends with the refrigerator and is used for COLD/HOT zone preparation as well as for small electrical appliances and the microwave oven built-in above.

The U shape surrounds a central island, which has become the primary preparation zone. As the cook works he can converse with a guest perched on a stool pulled up to the island or seated on the couch beyond. The island is located for easy pivoting between it and the sink or cooktop. On the cook's side of the island are open shelves, which make pulling out pots and pans easy, as well as an open alcove that holds buckets for garbage and recycling.

On one side of the couch is a cabinet that holds large serving pieces on one side and VCR tapes on the other. The kitchen edge of the couch area has built-in wine storage at cabinet level and open shelves above holding everyday and decorative china and pottery for easy access. Across from the couch in the central island the television has its hidden home.

Schwartz says he is still getting used to having enough space! He has to remind himself to work along the length of the island, since his necessity-honed habits of cramped preparation have made using expansive space a practice to be cultivated.

ABOVE LEFT: THE UNDERMOUNTED SINK WAS CUSTOM-MADE. NOTE THE CURVE CUT IN THE WOODEN WINDOWSILL TO ACCOMMODATE THE FAUCET. ABOVE CENTER: FACING INTO THE DINING ROOM IS A NARROW SET OF SHELVES DESIGNED TO HOLD SMALL ITEMS. ABOVE RIGHT: THE TELEVISION PULLS OUT OF A CABINET ON A RETRACTING SHELF. RIGHT: SPICES ARE STORED AROUND THE CORNER FROM THE STOVE IN A DRAWER FITTED WITH AN INSERT TO HOLD THEM EFFICIENTLY.

ED AND ELLIE GIOBBI

PAINTER, COOK, FARMER, AND AUTHOR ED GIOBBI LIVES WITH HIS wife, Ellie, in Westchester County, New York, in a pastoral setting that belies its proximity to New York City. Giobbi leads what must be one of the most well-integrated lives of anyone in the food business, a life that he has documented in his most recent cookbook, *Pleasures of the Good Earth*. In it, Giobbi details wonderful recipes based on the produce, poultry, and meat he raises and also gives ancillary instructions on winemaking, slaughtering, gardening, and cooking.

Giobbi's father came from the Marches region of Italy, and Giobbi was raised in Connecticut with a sound appreciation for the Italian traditions of his ancestry. His lifestyle today would still not be out of place in rural Italy, although it is certainly both sophisticated and soul-warming.

Giobbi's kitchen, which he and Ellie designed over twenty years ago, was one of the very first residential kitchens to have a restaurant stove installed in it. It had an enormous influence on other chefs and kitchen designers, who appreciated the stove's massive visual appeal as well as the strength of its burners.

Giobbi and his wife were ahead of their time as kitchen designers in other ways as well: when they added the study, dining area, and seating arrangements to their kitchen addition, they anticipated our current interest in the kitchen as great room/heart of the house.

The cooking area of the kitchen is only slightly changed since the Giobbis first bought the property. They added the wooden perpendicular preparation counter that divides the cooking area from the kitchen table, and they added

FAR LEFT: IN HIS SUBURBAN NEW YORK KITCHEN, ED GIOBBI HAS SITUATED THE RESTAURANT RANGE NEXT TO A MARBLE-TOPPED COUNTER FOR RESTING HOT POTS. COLOR IS USED IN THIS KITCHEN AS ART, TO ENLIVEN AND ACCENTUATE DIFFERENT AREAS. LEFT: ED GIOBBI BUILDS A FIRE IN THE OPEN FIREPLACE OF THE SITTING-ROOM AREA OF THE KITCHEN COMPLEX. THE MANTELPIECE IS AN ITALIAN ANTIQUE. BELOW: ED'S COOKBOOK-WRITING AND REFERENCE AREA IS OPPOSITE THE KITCHEN. ONE OF ED'S ROUND PAINTINGS HANGS ABOVE THE DINING TABLE.

the famous restaurant range that dominates the brick wall. Even now, they still find the cooking area to be quite functional (Ed does most of the cooking, and Ellie the baking), although Ed says that if he were renovating the kitchen today he might move the sink a little, to provide more counter space near the preparation area.

What dissatisfied them about their kitchen was the lack of social space. It was to this end that they added the dining area (set under a "duomo" skylight that illuminates Ed's painting), the sitting room, complete with an antique Italian mantel, and the alcove study for cookbook research and writing.

Although the expanded kitchen has clear architectural boundaries, the place of food in this household extends over other indoor and outdoor areas: porch and terrace provide dining areas, as does a table under an arbor supported by massive stone piers.

Two poultry houses grace the property—the one near Ellie's studio holds exotic birds for visual pleasure and affection, and the chicken house near the gardens holds poultry intended for future meals. Similarly, aside from the old and much-loved pet rabbit who, in his dotage, has the run of the vegetable garden, rabbits raised for meat are caged on the grounds.

The vegetable gardens hold an impressive array of foodstuffs, all raised with a year of fresh eating, canning, and freezing in mind. A root cellar on the property has been turned into a winery, where Giobbi and his son-in-law make wine for their families with grapes bought in bulk from California. And there is one cupboard in the pantry that is the epitome of the garden's promise—it is filled with rows of glowing, jewel-like jars of preserved home-grown tomatoes.

LEFT: NEXT TO THE STOVE, THE BRICK WALL IS COVERED WITH COPPER COOKWARE AND MOLDS. AN EAT-IN-THE-KITCHEN TABLE IS IN FRONT OF THE WINDOW. THE CHAIRS ARE ITALIAN ANTIQUES.

ABOVE LEFT: THE SHELVES IN THE NEARBY PANTRY ARE FILLED WITH HOME-GROWN AND HOME-CANNED PRODUCE AND TOOLS FOR ITALIAN CUISINE. ABOVE RIGHT: THE FORMER ROOT CELLAR IS NOW USED ANNUALLY FOR PRESSING, BOTTLING, AND STORING HOMEMADE WINE. THE BRONZE RELIEFS ON THE DOOR WERE MADE YEARS AGO BY THE GIOBBI CHILDREN. LEFT: INSIDE THE CELLAR, WINE RESTS IN CASKS AND BOTTLES, GETTING READY FOR A YEAR'S WORTH OF GOOD MEALS.

RESTAURANT CHEFS

TODD AND OLIVIA ENGLISH

TODD ENGLISH HAD STINTS AT LE CÔTE BASQUE IN NEW YORK AND Michaela's restaurant in Cambridge before starting his own restaurant, Olives, in 1989. Today, Olives has moved to larger quarters in the Charlestown section of Boston, and the original restaurant down the street has become Figs: in the evening a pasta-and-pizza restaurant, and by day a commercial brick-oven bread bakery. In the meantime Todd and his wife, Olivia, have become the parents of Oliver and Isabella and the owners of a town house near both restaurants.

The restaurant kitchen is in two parts—a large stainless-steel prep kitchen hidden from view, and the wood-fired kitchen, which is located at one end of the dining room.

LEFT: THE OPEN-TO-VIEW WOOD-FIRED KITCHEN AT OLIVES HAS A ROTISSERIE ON THE LEFT FOR SPIT COOKING, AND BELOW THAT, AN IRON GRID FOR GRILLING. THE WOOD-FIRED OVEN AT RIGHT IS USED FOR BAKING AND ROASTING MEATS AND VEGETABLES. RIGHT: THE ENGLISHES' HOME KITCHEN IS SEDATE, IN CONTRAST TO THEIR RESTAURANTS. THE CHERRY CABINETS WERE CUSTOM MADE TO TAKE ADVANTAGE OF THE FULL HEIGHT OF THE ROOM AND THE HEIGHT OF THE COOKS.

The wood-fired kitchen boasts a Todd English–designed rotisserie with three long removable spits that each can hold four or five chickens at a time, a large grill set over wood coals, and a classic brick oven used for dishes baked in clay. Each of these three fires is built separately (the restaurant uses a cord of wood about every ten days!) and the grill and oven are positioned high on two walls so that the fire is visible from every seat in the restaurant as well as through the windows on the street.

Todd, who does most of the wood cooking, has designed this station to fit his own tall scale and to make working at the wood-fire stations compact and efficient. He can reach everything he needs within three steps, from grill to oven to counter. A small cleanup sink has been fitted in beside the grill, and massive Pennsylvania slate counters ring the bar that divides the fireplaces from the diners. Suspended infrared heat lamps keep finished dishes warm as they are removed from the heat.

Olivia designed the interior of both restaurants, using new and salvaged antique materials to create a feeling of celebratory ease. She has been so successful in this endeavor that she has recently been asked to design other restaurants in the Boston area.

In contrast, their home kitchen is used by both chefs and is occupied as well by Oliver and their two dogs. Using many of the same elements as the restaurant, Todd and Olivia have created a space that is equally efficient but smaller in scale and warmer in feeling. At home the materials are more sensual: the stone countertops are polished granite instead of rough slate, and the cherry-wood cabinets are new

OPPOSITE, FAR LEFT: BREADS ARE BAKED IN THE BRICK OVENS DOWN THE STREET AT FIGS, WHICH IS BY DAY A BREAD BAK-ERY AND BY NIGHT A PIZZERIA. OPPOSITE, CENTER: TODD, OLIVIA, AND OLIVER AT HOME. OPPOSITE, RIGHT: THE CAVE AT OLIVES HOLDS BOTTLED WINES IN OLD WINE CASKS SECURED BEHIND AN ITALIAN-INSPIRED IRON GATE. BELOW LEFT: HAND-MADE PASTA DRIES ON A TRAY NEXT TO AN OLIVE-OIL JAR RECYCLED INTO A VASE FOR FLOWERS. BELOW RIGHT: THE DEEP ANTIQUE SOAPSTONE SINK IN THE HOME KITCHEN WEARS ITS PATINA PROUDLY. ABOVE IT, A WINDOW OFFERS A VIEW INTO THE BACK GARDEN.

examples of the cabinetmaker's art designed in classic style. The deep antique soap-stone sink, a lucky find in a Maine antiques store, forms a strong contrast with the state-of-the-art stainless-steel cooktop and oven, here arranged as if they were a one-piece range.

Many people, faced with designing a new kitchen in this space, would have brought the peninsula closer to the sink, leaving room on its other side for a table and chairs in front of the fire. The Englishes, with cooking first and foremost on their minds, chose instead to maximize the preparation areas and scale the work space for two chefs to work together. They eat at pull-up stools on the peninsula itself, or at a dining table in the adjoining living room.

One wall of the kitchen overlooking the back garden is allocated to the WET zone, with ample working space on both sides of the sink. Another wall is used for HOT zone work, with the peninsula opposite it functioning as preparation area for the COLD and DRY zones. A large floor-to-ceiling cupboard between the kitchen and living room doors functions as a pantry, and shelves on each side of the fireplace hold cookbooks, family memorabilia, and a television hidden behind closed doors.

On his rare days off from cooking at the restaurant, the wood-burning chef takes a busman's holiday in his domestic haven, grilling at the fireplace in winter and in the back yard in warm weather.

LEFT: ONE END OF THE KITCHEN HAS A FIREPLACE FOR INDOOR GRILLING, OR JUST FOR THE PLEASURE OF WATCHING THE FLAMES. THE CUPBOARD AT RIGHT HIDES A TELEVISION, ALONG WITH AN OVERFLOW OF COOKBOOKS FROM THE SHELVES AT LEFT.

JOHANNE KILLEEN AND GEORGE GERMON

JOHANNE KILLEEN AND GEORGE GERMON, PARTNERS IN LIFE AS WELL as in food, are the owners of Al Forno in Providence, Rhode Island. They are artist-graduates of the Rhode Island School of Design, and their involvement with food, which started as an avocation, turned into their profession.

George, whose background is in ceramics, designed and built the wood-fired kiln-like oven that gives its smoke-flavored signature to so many of their wonderful

meals. Centered in their open-to-view professional kitchen, which occupies about a quarter of the upstairs restaurant, it provides hungry customers with the sights and aromas of the "coming attractions" on the menu.

The restaurant kitchen is notable in other dimensions as well: it features a series of well-organized work stations that proceed down its length in two parallel rows. Each station is more-than-usually well defined, and the cooks within them are

completely responsible both for the food they prepare and the overall condition of the space. All of this aids the quality of the meals produced at Al Forno, as well as the smoothness of the restaurant's flow.

Johanne and George's home kitchen dominates the entire first floor of their living space, emphasizing the central position of food in both their private and public lives. Ranged against one long wall and one parallel short wall, it is a galley kitchen

with a twist—all the equipment is of massive and professional scale. This could be overwhelming, but they have used their artists' eyes to subdue the look of these commercial behemoths by surrounding them with soft color, subtle textures, and domestic-scale storage hidden behind glass doors.

As in the restaurant kitchen, each zone is clearly defined, allowing both cooks to work simultaneously without interference. The HOT zone is particularly impressive, both in size and in location, because the lavish stainless steel surrounding the range so dominates the space. Next to it, the fireplace functions as an auxiliary HOT zone for grilling and baking. The long wooden worktable that parallels the range provides a lower surface for DRY zone/COLD zone mixing and chopping, with storage underneath. Opposite the fireplace, a table for eight allows hosts and guests to admire the flames.

Looking at home and restaurant versions of kitchens used by the same cooks reminds us that the principles of kitchen design are the same, whether the space is small or large, private or public. Clarity of purpose, attention to detail, and planning are the cornerstones of any well-designed kitchen space.

LEFT: ARRANGED ABOVE THE WINDOWS IN THE DRY PREPARATION AREA IS AN ENVIABLE COLLECTION OF COPPER POTS. AT LEFT IS MORE COOKWARE IN A BRITISH POT RACK. ABOVE: JOHANNE KILLEEN AT THE OUTDOOR SINK, ARRANGING FLOWERS FOR THE TABLE.

CATERERS

SHARON MYERS

SHARON MYERS FINE CATERING IS RUN FROM A MODEST HOME kitchen. Although the architecture and layout are virtually unchanged from the time of her original purchase, Sharon made enormous changes in the functionality of the kitchen. She invested in the best equipment she could afford, she eliminated some conventional eat-in arrangements to make room for preparation and storage spaces, and she disguised what was left with color and style. Her kitchen is a lesson in using what you have with intelligence, a useful reminder that an extremely hardworking kitchen can be created with a minimum of expense.

She began by tearing out a built-in breakfront and a closet on each side of the bay window, making room for more efficient open-shelf storage on one side and a six-burner professional range and exhaust system on the other. The central space in front of the bay window, which had previously held a dining table and chandelier, is now occupied by the sturdy worktable Sharon had made to her specifications, which stores large mixing bowls and baking equipment on a low open shelf beneath its butcher-block top.

The floor was originally covered with wall-to-wall carpeting, which Sharon removed. She painted the plywood subfloor in a patchwork pattern of pink and lavender. The existing cabinets, which were dark varnished pine in a standard suburban neo-Colonial style, were coated with a sticks-to-anything primer (BIN) and then painted with a soft-white enamel. Hinges and pulls were replaced for a more modern look, and an ugly wooden valance was removed from above the sink window. The ceiling was painted pale pink-lilac, which casts a warm glow on food and cooks, and the adjacent hallway walls were colored a sympathetic deeper lavender.

PAGE 135: SHARON MYERS USES THE RESTAURANT RANGE AT LEFT FOR COOKING; THE ELECTRIC RANGE IS USED ONLY FOR AUXILIARY BAKING. OPPOSITE, TOP LEFT: THE BASEMENT PANTRY STORES STAPLES AND CONTAINERS. OPPOSITE, TOP RIGHT: THE KITCHEN'S ORIGINAL PENINSULA IS STILL IN PLACE, BUT IT HAS BEEN PAINTED AND TOPPED WITH BUTCHER BLOCK. OPPOSITE, BOTTOM: THIS MASSIVE AND STURDY CUSTOM-MADE WORKTABLE IS THE SINGLE MOST USEFUL PIECE IN THIS KITCHEN. ABOVE LEFT: TOOLS FOR COOKING LINE THE END OF THE WORKTABLE NEAREST THE STOVE. ABOVE CENTER: CATERERS NEED MULTIPLE PANS FOR MULTIPLE COOKS. ABOVE RIGHT: PASTRY BRUSHES, SPATULAS, WHISKS, AND WOODEN SPOONS HAVE THEIR OWN CONTAINERS IN ROWS ALONG THE WINDOWSILL.

RIGHT: SHARON MYERS AT WORK, WITH FLOWERS FROM HER GARDEN.

A considerably larger and better-quality stainless-steel double sink was installed, along with new laminate counters that followed the lines of the original countertops. Pale-pink ceramic tile was used to line the wall around the stove and exhaust hood for ease in cleaning. The original electric stove's oven is used as an auxiliary baking oven, and the top of the electric stove has been covered with laminate to increase the amount of counter space available. (The controls for the now-hidden stovetop burners have been turned off.)

Because this is a kitchen from which meals for up to five hundred people at a time are prepared by a cooking crew, all preparation tools and equipment are stored accessibly along open shelves or on wall grids or hung from ceiling beams. A large open basement below the kitchen holds backup pantry items and bulk food supplies, five additional refrigerators and an auxiliary freezer, transport and storage containers, baskets, and specialized pots and pans.

The kitchen functions efficiently for multiple cooks (as well as one cook working alone) because the work zones are clearly defined—the generous sink (WET zone) is divided, allowing the side near the dishwasher to be used for cleanup, and the side near the refrigerator to be used for food washing and preparation. HOT is a clearly defined zone (set, unfortunately, into a corner) that provides room for one person to work at stove and oven, turning to the adjacent island/worktable for additional counter space as needed. Most of the worktable functions as a food-preparation zone, and holds machines for mixing and chopping. As many as three people can work at various stations around the worktable, thanks to its central placement, which allows passage around all four sides. Finally, the kitchen's original peninsula parallel to the worktable allows yet another cook to do DRY or COLD preparation work (it is also convenient to the refrigerator in the kitchen and is the shortest distance to the auxiliary cold storage downstairs).

This working cook's kitchen also functions well because it is so heavily used. If the open arrangements of implements and pots and pans were merely decorative, they would always be dusty, but because everything is in nearly constant use (and because the kitchen is professionally cleaned on a regular basis), every tool is ready to be removed and plunged into service.

NANCY POLSENO

NANCY POLSENO'S CATERING FIRM, THE BARKING RADISH, WAS BORN in her original home kitchen, which occupied only a fraction of the space her redesigned kitchen takes up today. After two and a half years of increasingly successful events, Nancy felt it was time to make her kitchen more compatible with her business. She consulted with Denny Frehsee, a designer who specializes in kitchens, and then devoted her considerable organizational abilities to planning a kitchen that would meet the professional requirements of a six-person catering team, as well as her family of four.

It is a marvel of planning. Every drawer (and there are twenty-two altogether) is organized into sub-baskets of related tools that are all used for a particular function. Thus, the drawer under the marble baking center (COLD zone, DRY zone) holds rolling pins of every variety, pastry cutters, and a variety of measuring spoons and

PREVIOUS PAGE: NANCY POLSENO HAS ORGANIZED HER KITCHEN FOR MAXIMUM EFFICIENCY. THE CENTRAL ISLAND IS ON THE LEFT, WITH A SINK AT THE FAR END; THE BAKING STATION IS ON THE OTHER SIDE OF THE SINK, AND THE MASSIVE OLD RESTAURANT RANGE IS CENTERED AMONG THE CABINETS ON THE RIGHT: ABOVE LEFT: THE BAKING STATION HAS A MARBLE INSERT, AND IS LOWER IN HEIGHT THAN THE SURROUNDING CABINETS. ABOVE CENTER: SERVING-PLATTER STORAGE TAKES UP TWO WHOLE BASE CABINETS. THE MOST FRAGILE PLATES ARE CUSHIONED WITH THIN FOAM SLABS. ABOVE RIGHT: KNIVES ARE STORED UNOBTRUSIVELY BETWEEN BASE CABINETS IN SLOTS CUT THROUGH THE BUTCHER BLOCK OF THE CENTRAL ISLAND. BELOW: AS SEEN FROM THE DINING END OF THE KITCHEN, THE BAKING CENTER IS AT LEFT, AND THE UNUSUAL END-ISLAND LOCATION OF THE SINK IS VISIBLE. THE DISHWASHER IS AROUND THE CORNER FROM THE SINK. RIGHT: THE MASSIVE STAINLESS-STEEL REFRIGERATOR IS A COMMERCIAL MODEL, AND IS LOCATED IN AN ALCOVE NEAR THE ISLAND.

cups. The cupboard beneath has a shelf that rolls out to reveal mixing bowls, flour and sugar stores, and all auxiliary baking-preparation equipment. On an adjacent (and higher) counter, both a portable mixer and a large stand mixer wait at the ready.

Similarly, the central island was designed with storage that efficiently anticipates the many functions the island serves within the room. (Although bulk food storage takes up the pantry and basement, often-used ingredients are kept in the kitchen.) The side of the island that is opposite the stove stores ingredients on pull-out shelves devoted (on one side) only to savory oils and vinegars, and (in the next-door cabinet) a shelf of staple canned goods. The stack of drawers holds utensils, peelers and graters, and blades for the Cuisinart above. This side of the island functions both as a general food-preparation zone and as a HOT preparation zone in conjunction with the stove. It is the primary cooking station in the kitchen, whether for family or profes-

sional use. All oven and stove-top equipment is stored next to the stove either on pullout shelves or suspended along the rack above. The passage between island and stove is wide enough so that it works both for solo work or as two work stations.

The opposite side of the island functions similarly, in that it can work either as one or two separate preparation zones (DRY, COLD) independently or in conjunction with its opposite appliance, the commercial refrigerator. Storage on this side of the island is for silverware and napkins as well as family snacks—nuts, crackers, breads, and nut butters. Above the island, and accessible from both sides, are everyday plates and glassware. This station is also

LEFT: EACH DRAWER OF THIS ANTIQUE CHEST HOLDS GROUPS OF RELATED TOOLS—SPOONS ARE IN ONE DRAWER AND TINY BRASS CANDLEHOLDERS IN THE OTHER. ABOVE: SPICES AND STAPLES ARE STORED IN MATCHING JARS THAT ONCE WERE HOME TO MAYONNAISE (THE LARGE ONES) AND IMPORTED JAMS (THE SMALL ONES).

used in conjunction with the refrigerator and sink by the catering staff for preparation of crudités.

The most unusual element in the island is the end location of the large commercial sink. This placement was Nancy's idea, and she still feels satisfied with the efficiency of her plan. Because of the sink's unusual location, it is accessible from both sides of the island as well as the sink end, making it work for three or four different work stations. (It is located opposite the baking area.) There are some disadvantages to this location, however: there is no real place to stack or drain dishes, except in one of the sinks, and as there is no backsplash, splashes are not always contained within the WET area. Nevertheless, this kind of central sink location does offer some of the advantages of two sinks with less expense and fewer square feet requirements.

Opposite the sink, at the other end of the island, is yet another work station used for chopping. The person who works at this end does preliminary preparation for cooks at other stations when the kitchen is operating in its catering mode.

Another of Nancy's good ideas is the double cabinet holding a large collection of serving platters vertically. Although tray cupboards are not uncommon, it would be difficult in a conventional kitchen to store such a variety of flat, shallow ware without nesting it. Nancy's solution works well for her and is a useful model for others.

This kitchen works for Nancy because she knew herself, her cooking patterns, and exactly what activities would occur within the different parts of the space. By spending months on the planning in conjunction with her architect, imagining herself working in the room, Nancy was able to create a kitchen that is well tailored to the needs of all who cook there.

BELOW: COLOR-CODED PLASTIC BASKETS ORDER EACH KIND OF TOOL. BOTTOM: A CUT-METAL SCULPTURE BY GENNARO PROZZO SERVES AS INSPIRATION. BELOW RIGHT: NANCY POLSENO AT WORK. NOTE THE PLACEMENT OF THE COUNTER IN RELATION TO HER HEIGHT. FOLLOWING PAGE: HOMEGROWN FLOWERS AND VEGETABLES DISPLAY SUMMER'S PLENTY.

□

PART THREE

KITCHEN SOURCE GUIDE

...

PRODUCTS & RESOURCES

PROFESSIONAL SOURCES

SPECIALTY COOKERS

AGA
RFD 1, Box 477
Stowe, VT 05672
(802) 253-9727
Always-on range/cooker.

TULIKIVI
The New Alberene Stone Co.
P.O. Box 300
Schuyler, VA 22969
(804) 831-2228
Finnish-style soapstone
heaters and cookers, some
with bake ovens.

CONVECTION-COMBINATION OVENS

GROEN
1900 Pratt Boulevard
Elk Grove Village, IL 60007
(708) 439-2400
Combination convection/
steam oven for commercial use.

Blodgett

BLODGETT
Blodgett Oven Company
50 Lakeside Avenue
Box 788
Burlington, VT 05402-0788
(802) 658-6600
Combination
convection/steam oven for
commercial use.

Groen

WOOD-FIRED OVENS

EARTHSTONE
Earthstone Wood-Fired
Ovens
237 S. La Brea Avenue
Los Angeles, CA 90036
(213) 656-5926
French wood-fired ovens for
home and commercial use.

Earthstone Model 90

RENATO
Renato Woodburning/Gas
Brick Ovens/Rotisseries
Renato Specialty Products
11350 Pagemill
Dallas, TX 75243
(214) 349-5296
Wood- and gas-burning
specialty ovens.

Renato

BARBECUE EQUIPMENT

J & R
J & R Manufacturing, Inc.
P.O. Box 850522
Mesquite, TX 75185-0522
(214) 285-4855
Commercial and residential
barbecues.

WEBER GRILLS
Weber-Stephen Products
Company
200 East Daniels Road
Palatine, IL 60067
(708) 934-5700

Residential barbecues and
home smokers.

Weber Grill

COOKING EQUIPMENT

DACOR
950 South Raymond Avenue
Pasadena, CA 91109
(818) 305-7616
Residential cooking equipment.

FIVE STAR
Brown Stove Works, Inc.
P.O. Box 2490
Cleveland, TN 37320
(615) 476-6544 or
(800) 251-7485
Crossover pro-style ranges.

Five Star

GAGGENAU
425 University Avenue
Norwood, MA 02062
(617) 255-1766
Residential ranges, ovens,
cooktops.

Gaggenau

GARLAND
Garland Commercial
Industries
185 East South Street
Freeland, PA 18224
(717) 636-1000
Commercial and crossover
ranges.

RUSSELL RANGE
325 South Maple Avenue #5
South San Francisco, CA
94080
(415) 873-0105
Crossover pro-style ranges,
cooktops.

Russell Range

THERMADOR
5119 District Boulevard
P.O. Box 22129
Los Angeles, CA 90022
(800) 656-9226
Quality, residential, and professionally inspired ovens, ranges, ventilation equipment. Also dishwashers and trash compactors.

Thermador

VIKING
Viking Range Corporation
P.O. Drawer 956
111 Front Street
Greenwood, MS 38930
(601) 455-1200
Crossover residential pro-style ranges.

Viking Range

WOLF
Wolf Range Company
19600 S. Alameda Street
Compton, CA 90221
(310) 637-3737
Crossover and professional ranges.

Wolf Range

REFRIGERATORS

SUB-ZERO
P.O. Box 44130
Madison, WI 53744-4130
(608) 271-2233
Twenty-four-inch-deep pro-style residential refrigerators.

TRAULSEN
114-02 15th Avenue
College Pt. NY 11356
(718) 463-9000
Manufacturers of commercial and residential/crossover refrigerators, wine racks, freezers.

KITCHEN CABINETS AND INTERIOR FITTINGS

IKEA
Ikea USA Headquarters
Plymouth Meeting Mall
Plymouth Meeting, PA
19462
(215) 834-0150
Other stores in Pittsburgh, PA; Baltimore, MD; Elizabeth, NJ; Woodbridge, VA; Hicksville, NY; Houston, TX. Swedish-designed Euro-style kitchen cabinets and Rationell wire-coated interior fittings.

Ikea cabinet & wire-coated fittings

ELFA
300-3A Route 17 South
Lodi, NJ 07644
(201) 777-1554
Swedish-made coated-wire storage.

PLACEWARES
Corporate Headquarters:
344 Vanderbilt Avenue
Norwood, MA 02062
Chain of retail stores in the Boston area specializing in storage aids and space planning.

PROFESSIONAL-STYLE TOOLS

Chef's Choice

CHEF'S CHOICE
EdgeCraft Corporation
P.O. Box 3000
Limestone and Southwood
Road
Avondale, PA 19311-0915
(800) 342-3255
American-made
professional-quality Trizor™
Professional 10X™ cutlery
knives; Chef's Choice™
Diamond Hone Knife™
Sharpener.

WUSTHOF-TRIDENT OF AMERICA
525 Executive Boulevard
P.O. Box 445
Elmsford, NY 10523-0445
(914) 347-2185
Professional-quality knives
in a wide range of sizes
and styles.

PROFESSIONALLY INSPIRED COOKWARE

ALL-CLAD
All-Clad Metal Crafters, Inc.
R.D. 2
Canonsburg, PA 15317
(412) 745-8300
Heavy aluminum pro-style
cookware lined with stainless steel, with copper,
aluminum, or stainless-steel
exteriors.

CALPHALON
Commercial Aluminum
Cookware Company
P.O. Box 583
Toledo, Ohio 43693
(419) 666-8700
Quality line of heavy-
duty aluminum cookware
first made for professional
use.

PROFESSIONAL STYLE AT RETAIL AND BY MAIL

A & J DISTRIBUTORS
236 Hanover
Boston, MA 02113
(617) 523-8490
Tools and equipment for
Italian cooking.

ALBERT USTER IMPORTS
Professional Chef's Tool
Catalog
9211 Gaither Road
Gaithersburg, MD 20877
(301) 258-7350
Professional equipment for
cooking, baking, and
decorating.

BROADWAY PANHANDLER
520 Spring Street
New York, NY 10012
(212) 966-3434
Retail store for
cookware.

BRIDGE KITCHENWARE COMPANY
214 E. 52nd Street
New York, NY 10022
(212) 688-4220
Retail cookware and
equipment; huge
inventory.

COMMERCIAL CULINARY
P.O. Box 30010
Alexandria, VA 22310
(800) 999-4949
Mail-order source
for professionally
inspired cookware at
a discount.

EUROPEAN HOME PRODUCTS
Order Department
P.O. Box 2524
Waterbury, CT 06723
(800) 225-0760
Discounted fine tools and
accessories.
Retail Store
236 East Avenue
Norwalk, CT 06855

LA CUISINE
323 Cameron Street
Alexandria, VA 22314
(800) 521-1176
Extensive inventory of
imported cookware.

MAID OF SCANDINAVIA
3244 Raleigh Avenue
Minneapolis, MN 55416
(800) 328-6722
Source for baking pans
and supplies.

SUR LA TABLE
84 Pine Street
Pike Place Farmers' Market
Seattle, WA 98101
(800) 243-0852
Quality cookware and
supplies.

WILLIAMS-SONOMA
Mail Order Department
P.O. Box 7456
San Francisco, CA
94120-7456
(800) 541-2233
Mail-order supplies for cooks.

GREEN SOURCES

COMPOSTING

GREEN CONE
Box 866
Menlo Park, CA 94126
(415) 365-8637
Food-waste digester that
works on solar energy.

KEMP COMPOST TUMBLER
160 Koser Road
Lititz, PA 17543
(717) 626-5600
Makes compost more rapidly
than still methods, by agitat-
ing the compost in a crank-
turned composting barrel.

WORM COMPOSTING

WORMS EAT MY GARBAGE
($10.50)
Flower Press
10332 Shaver Road
Kalamazoo, MI 49002
(616) 327-0108
Sold by the author, Mary
Appelhof, who also sells the
"Worm-a-way" aerated worm
bin (same address).

Worm-a-way composter

MAIL-ORDER GREEN SUPPLIES

GARDENER'S SUPPLY
128 Intervale Road
Burlington, VT 05401
Mail-order source for wide
range of Green supplies and
equipment, including a variety of compost containers
and methods.

RECYCLING/SORTING

POLDER
200 Central Park Avenue
P.O. Box 456
Hartsdale, NY 10530
(914) 683-3733
Manufacturer of receptacles
for sorting trash.

ENVIRONMENTALLY FRIENDLY MATERIAL

SYNDECRETE
Syndesis
2908 Colorado Avenue
Santa Monica, CA 90404
(310) 829-9932
Cement and recycled mate-
rial concrete composite
designed to be custom-cast
and used for countertops,
sinks, flooring.

NONASBESTOS LINOLEUM

KROMMENIC LINOFLEX TILE KROMMENIC SHEET LINOLEUM
Forbo North America
(800) 842-7839
for local distributors
New England region:
Parkwood New England
13163 Mystic Valley
Parkway
Medford, MA 02155
Nonasbestos linoleum
flooring made with linseed
oil, cork, wood flour, resin
binders, dry pigments.

GREEN INFORMATION SOURCES

ENVIRONMENTAL
BUILDING NEWS
R.R. 1, Box 161
Brattleboro, VT 05301
Bimonthly newsletter; subscription $60/year.

BUILDING WITH NATURE
P.O. Box 369
Gualala, CA 95445

Bimonthly newsletter; subscription $45/year.

ENERGY SOURCE
DIRECTORY: A GUIDE
TO PRODUCTS USED IN
ENERGY-EFFICIENT
CONSTRUCTION
($175)
Iris Communications, Inc.
P.O. Box 1647
Tualatin, OR 97062
(503) 620-0881

This unique information source is extremely useful for builders who construct many projects.

PROFESSIONAL ORGANIZATIONS

NKBA
National Kitchen and
Bath Association
687 Willow Grove Street
Hackettstown, NJ 07840
Publishes a free state-by-state directory of members; aids consumers in finding qualified kitchen and bathroom designers.

IACP
International Association of
Culinary Professionals
304 West Liberty Street,
Suite 201
Louisville, KY 40202
(502) 581-9786
Publishes newsletter and directory of members, holds annual convention.

USEFUL BOOKS

BETTER KITCHENS,
by Cecile Shapiro, David Ulrich, and Neal DeLeo.
Passaic, NJ: Creative Homeowners Press, 1980.

CLEAN AND GREEN,
by Annie Berthold-Bond
Woodstock, NY: Ceres Press, 1990.

COMPLETE BOOK OF KITCHEN DESIGN,
by Ellen Rand, Florence Perchuk, and the editors of Consumer Reports Books
Yonkers, NY: Consumer Reports Books, 1991.

DOWN TO EARTH GARDENING KNOW HOW FOR THE 90's,
by Dick Raymond
Pownal, VT: Storey Publishing, 1991.

KITCHENS,
a volume in Rodale's Home Design Series,
by the editors of Rodale's *New Shelter* magazine
Emmaus, PA: Rodale Press, 1986.

PLANNING THE PERFECT KITCHEN,
by Bo Niles and Juta Ristsoo
New York: Simon & Schuster, 1988.

SMALL KITCHENS,
by Robin Murrell
New York: Simon & Schuster, 1986.

STEP BY STEP ORGANIC VEGETABLE GARDENING,
by Shepherd Ogden
New York: Harper Collins, 1992.

THE COOKS' CATALOGUE,
by Beard, Glaser, Wolf Ltd.
New York: Harper & Row, 1975.

THE HOUSE BOOK,
by Terence Conran
New York: Crown, 1982.

THE WELL-TOOLED KITCHEN,
by Fred Bridge and Jean F. Tibbetts
New York: William Morrow, 1991.

THIS OLD HOUSE KITCHENS,
by Steve Thomas and Philip Langdon
Boston: Little, Brown, 1992.

THE SMART KITCHEN,
by David Goldbeck
Woodstock, NY: Ceres Press, 1989.